Managing Marginal or Incompetent Staff

A Practical Guide

Managing Marginal or Incompetent Staff

A Practical Guide

Jo Campbell

CAMBRIA
PRESS

Youngstown, New York

This book has been registered with the Library of Congress.
Campbell, Jo,
        Supervising Marginal or Incompetent Staff/Jo Campbell
        p. cm.
        Includes bibliographical references
        0-9773567-4-4

DISCLAIMER

This information is provided with the understanding that the author and publisher are not engaged in offering legal services. The author and publisher disclaim any liability, loss or risk incurred as a consequence of this information. This information is not a substitute for the advice of a competent human resources person or legal professional.

DEDICATION

This book is dedicated to all the educators who have passed through my life throughout my career. Thank you to almost all of them for their mentorship and modeling. More importantly, thank you for being there for the kids!

TABLE OF CONTENTS

Managing Marginal or Incompetent Staff

A Practical Guide

FOREWORD

Life is full of difficult people, situations and demands but we never quite learn to deal with them. Although we have many, many school employees who are dedicated, productive, and positive thinkers, I'm sure you'll agree that we also have our share of whiners, tattlers, gossipers, complainers, and people who refuse to or are unable to do the job as well as required for our children to grow into respectful and productive adults. Successful administrators must take a tough line with difficult employees who are choosing to allow their negative attitudes and behaviors to impact the children whose lives we place in their hands. These employees also have the power of lowering staff morale and upsetting all who have to work along side them.

The reason we have difficult people in the work place is that we allow them to behave in this manner - in fact, we reward them by overlooking inappropriate behavior, giving them less responsibility, placing "marginal" children in their care whose parents are least likely to complain and the most important reward of all...a paycheck! A paycheck tells an employee, "Good job, so good that we'd like to share several thousand dollars of our district's money with you."

Why do we allow and even reward difficult people? Because, unfortunately, most managers do not have the experience, courage or motivation to do what is necessary to "take on" a difficult person. These people are indeed masters of their game. And it is a game. Just how much can they get away with before they meet the person with the skills, knowledge, and commitment to either change and improve the negative behaviors or successfully counsel the employee to change to a profession where children aren't affected by their choices.

This book is a very clear guide to helping managers deal with the difficult employee and set the standards and goals necessary for them to create a healthy, functional workplace where employees treat themselves, their colleagues and most importantly the children in a respectful manner. This is a guide to restoring and maintaining healthy, positive attitudes and behaviors in the work place. I recommend this guide to every manager and administrator as essential reading. Our children are indeed our most important resource - they always deserve the best we can give, especially when it comes to the role models we place before them.

Connie Podesta, M.S., LPC, CSP
Dallas, Texas

PREFACE

This year, I have met a major milestone in my career, twenty-nine years in education! It sounds even more impressive when it is stated that it is more than a quarter of a CENTURY! (At least to me.)

Throughout the years that have evaporated far too quickly, I have had the privilege of working with tremendous teachers and administrators. When thinking back, so many of them were considered by me to be in the upper 10% so I know there are thousands of people who have passed through my life who have dedicated their careers to helping our new generations develop and who are exceptional, not marginal.

There have been a few educators that caused a great deal of concern and this book is written due to my belief that as an administrator, you have to be able to deal with the very small number of staff who are in the bottom 10%. It is such a difficult chore so I write this book to offer assistance in that endeavor.

When deciding to write this book, there were a number of people who encouraged me and who helped me through the process. First of all, had not a colleague, Connie Podesta, suggested it, I would not have thought of writing this book. She saw the work that I had generated for new administrators in our district on marginal staff and insisted that I write this book.

Close friends and family have been there to always support and encourage me. I thank them for being there for me throughout this book and throughout my life.

INTRODUCTION

The quality of teaching is the single most important factor affecting academic growth for students. It can make a significant difference in a student's life, let alone their test scores. The lasting effects of ignoring marginal or incompetent staff are immense. As administrators, it is one of the most important responsibilities to see that people who do not make a contribution to the district goals not be a part of the staff.

In today's educational climate it is even more important to address concerns with personnel for without the best and the brightest in the schools across the country the myriad of goals set before public education will not be met. As accountability for achievement becomes standard in every state, systems to help administrators deal with employees in need of improvement are essential.

Even though the tasks involved with working with marginal or incompetent staff often overwhelm administrators, it is essential to make the expectation to handle these concerns a part of the supervision and evaluation process.

It is against an educational leader's temperament to deal with incompetent or marginal staff. Most educators are trained to be positive, to take great pride in educational skills, and to be giving people. Educators have often been described as compassionate people who do not have the nature to work with misconduct in other professionals. Educators are taught to coach and mentor others. The idea of writing devastating evaluations, suggesting someone has failed or not supporting someone is the opposite of how most educators prefer to behave. There is no joy in it.

The effect of not dealing with incompetence is much greater than the unpleasant task of dealing with it. It is unlikely that any administrator has died from documentation, but they will likely feel the effects, for documentation is the pivotal aspect in successfully dealing with marginal or incompetent staff.

Observation and the resulting documentation need to be handled in a non-emotional manner. Keep in mind that it is *their* problem that you are attempting to solve. The calmer an administrator is during the process, the better it is for all concerned. There will be many times when dealing with marginal or incompetent staff that the word calm will not be the first one to come to mind but it is important for the success of the effort to stay personally not involved as much as the situation allows.

The administrator working with marginal or incompetent staff needs to consider his or her health and stay calm. Live to fight another day. Remember that you are doing what is expected of you and serving the higher goal of helping students learn and grow.

There is a major difference between the willingness of a staff member to succeed and his / her willingness to exert effort to improve his / her skills. The goal of working with marginal staff is to get them to want to work hard and in doing so make a difference in the area in which they are hired. They need to develop confidence in their own ability to change but first they must realize that there is a need to change. Creating this recognition is the first barrier that must be overcome to help them.

A system of timely, specific, and genuine criteria based on feedback is important to the overall success of staff supervision and evaluation. An administrator's attention and acknowledgement of effort and success impact the staff member's motivation. It is important to recognize and support staff effort to improve. The ultimate goal is not to "get rid of" staff but to help them improve their skills.

Truely marginal or incompetent staff members represent less than ten percent of the people managed in a career. Keep in mind that efforts to help them grow and sustain this growth is important not only for humanitarian reasons but also for the financial health of the district. It costs a great deal to recruit, hire, induct and mentor new staff.

Administrators need support and guidance when dealing with marginal or incompetent staff. Hopefully, this book will offer some ideas and assist in that task. To begin, a list of survival tips are offered to supervisors. They are as follows:

- Know that you were hired to be the instructional leader, not a social worker or a punching bag.
- Insist on improvement and don't accept excuses.
- Be direct and clear in your expectations.
- Be consistent, treating like issues alike.

- Be consistent in record keeping for good and bad performance.
- Observe often and document, document, document.
- Deal with the facts, be honest, and non-biased.
- Ask for help: Personnel, Attorney, and Assistant Superintendent.

Wouldn't it be nice if everyone got out of bed every morning with the intention of doing the very best they could in their positions with every expectation of success? Wouldn't it be nice if everyone working in an organization had the skill level appropriate for the tasks at hand? Wouldn't it be nice if every teacher, every classified person and every administrator had the willingness and commitment to accomplish the myriad of tasks necessary to run schools in a high quality manner?

Unfortunately, even though it would be nice, it just isn't so.

For a variety of reasons, people choose unsuitable careers. Some people stay in careers or positions just because it is a job that pays the bills. Other people stay in positions even though they hate what they are doing but see no way out. More serious are those people who do not even recognize that they are unhappy or unfulfilled in their positions. The most damaging people in our organizations are those who know that they are hurting others around them and either want to continue these behaviors for cruel reasons or because they are psychologically damaged and do not understand the seriousness of their actions.

Change is very difficult for many people. The thought of the need to change or being placed in the uncomfortable position of doing something else is beyond their capacity to consider. For some people, staying in a known, even uncomfortable situation is much safer than venturing forth to pursue the unknown. They may know that they are incompetent and recognize that they do not enjoy going to work every day and yet they may see no way out of the choices they have made.

Impact of Incompetence

For every marginal or incompetent staff member in our educational organizations there are literally hundreds of people who are affected by that person. The impact of marginal or incompetent staff can be felt for generations. It is not unusual for some parents to demand that their child not have a certain teacher because *they* had that teacher as a child and declared decades ago that they would never let their child be treated as they were. Other parents make similar demands on the basis of a rumor concerning a child who had experienced difficulty with a teacher. It could be as simple as their neighbor telling them of an experience their son or daughter had with that staff member.

It is often stated that when a parent sends their child to school, most of them want only the very best people around that child to help them grow and become all they can be without ridicule or incompetence hindering their success. Few parents want anything but the best for their children.

This is true of educators as well. When considering an incompetent staff member, one should ask whether one would want one's own children to interact with that person. This could be a very good barometer when deciding whether action should be taken.

The reputation of that particular school is in jeopardy when marginal or incompetent staff members are allowed to continue working in that environment. Those who have worked in education know how some schools have tremendously supportive community members while other schools are seen with much less confidence. Justified or not, the perceptions of the parents and public around a particular school are crucial to the success of that school. School buildings can be closed and staffs could be dispersed or let go if a building fails to serve the community in an appropriate fashion.

Another huge impact is the reputation of teaching and education in general. In times of great turmoil in education it takes little to fan the fires of disrespect for educators. If teachers encourage marginal and incompetent staff to continue they are impacting their effectiveness and their own personal reputations. They are hurting the professional status they have worked so hard to attain.

When marginal or incompetent staff are not confronted, the performance of even the most committed staff members is affected. After all, why should a qualified staff member fulfill all the expectations of their profession when the incompetent person working next door to them barely shows up for work, performs poorly and yet collects the same paycheck? The old adage of one rotten apple spoiling all in the barrel applies to incompetent staff. Even the most committed staff will eventually grow tired of "mopping up" after incompetent staff and be hurt by this incompetence in their own careers as their own motivation is stifled.

Students' lives are forever impacted by incompetent staff. It has been said that the impact of incompetent or poor teaching is hard to overcome after one year and nearly impossible if experienced over a longer period of time. This negative impact can last for generations. Imagine the high school student who has witnessed year after year of teachers working from yellow lesson plans and sitting behind a desk while the students sit in rows and read from a text. Think of those students as they grow into adulthood and are asked to support public educational bond issues or levies. Why would they be supportive? They may have developed a suspicion or possibly even a disgust with public education because of the personal experiences that they had with incompetent staff.

What about the parents of our students who experience marginal or incompetent staff? Beyond just citizens who vote, they are people who one would hope would support public education for their children. If more and more people choose to take their children out of public education in America, public education, as we know it, will no longer exist. Those hard working, dedicated educators will be working for private industry where schools will have control over who attends and what is taught. It is paramount to isolationism. It will likely change the entire fabric of the United States which is unique due to its free and appropriate public educational system. This system is very unique in the world and is the basis of the freedom that this country enjoys and celebrates.

Incompetent and marginal staff also impact the administrator who must devote resources to their management and supervision. The impact is great not only in time and energy but emotionally as well. Yet this task is far too important to ignore. Now, more than ever before, problems with marginal and incompetent staff must be addressed. The health of our educational system is at stake.

Who Are These People?

It would be great if a typical snapshot of the incompetent staff member could be provided. If such a picture were available, the administrator could simply walk up and down the hallways and recognize the signs. Unfortunately, it is not that easy. Some people in need of help are a great deal more apparent than others. There are "closet" marginal staff who perform barely to expectations when watched but regress to unacceptable behavior once the spotlight is off them.

In the educational environment marginal staff can be administrators, teachers, associates, cooks, custodians and coaches. Sometimes the people needing assistance are colleagues with whom one may have worked for many years. Other times, concerns became apparent when the administrator starts tenure at a new building.

Unfortunately, in some districts, the marginal staff issue is handled by moving such staff from one building to another that has less parental involvement so that complaints may lessen. This is clearly an unacceptable tactic if the district expects competence and commitment from their staff.

The movement from one building to the next is also an avoidance technique used by those who do not want to take on the responsibility of the handling their own personnel concerns. Some administrators may believe that if placed in a different environment, marginal staff will "heal" themselves. There may be some of truth to this but only if the marginal staff person understands that there is a need to grow and change. Normally that is not the case and the incompetent behavior continues and becomes more enforced in the new environment.

"Burying" the marginal and incompetent staff members in a particular building with less likelihood of complaints is a sad practice that also encourages the view that some buildings and students have greater value than others. Encouraging these kind of perceptions is demeaning and wrong.

Marginal or incompetent staff members need to be given the opportunity to improve or consider starting a different career. Such individuals are usually identified through good observation by administrators who take instructional leadership seriously. In addition, they are sometimes identified because of parental or other outside complaints.

Districts that have strong induction and mentorship programs with supervision models that expect and monitor excellence have fewer concerns than districts that are more lax in these areas. The creation of strong supervision and management programs is critical because it is much easier to recognize incompetence and deal with it early on rather than after an employee has tenure.

An administrator new to a building often does not want to start marginal staff proceedings the first year due to the fact that they could be labeled as "out to get staff." The administrator who chooses to ignore incompetent or marginal staff the first year they are in a building loses the opportunity to make that first impression of expectation of excellence for that building. They need to consider what impressions they have made if they choose to ignore behavior. It is much more effective to establish a core expectation for the building when the administrator is new to that facility. It is much harder to change perceptions later.

Cases and examples of marginal or incompetent staff behavior are varied and multifacted. They can be extremely obvious or they may become apparent only after a period of years. Examples of anonymous marginal or incompetent staff behavior are now presented.

Example 1

A teacher who had worked for a district for 30+ years was known by the students for her extreme emotional instability.

The effect of that knowledge was for the students to work in concert to try to get her to cry at least once per day. The administrator knew this was happening and the way he handled it was to meet with her out in the hallway while she was crying to try to give support. During those times in the hallway the class members sat in their desks, "behaving." Not once during that semester did the administrator observe the classroom or walk in unannounced to see what was happening.

Students in that class continually barraged the teacher with questions that totally took her off track. Due to the fact that she had not established a routine for that class that was conducive to learning, this went on day after day, year after year, and decade after decade.

A new administrator was assigned to the building and began dropping into this class. He took the responsibility of classroom observation seriously, witnessed the class behavior and was able to talk with the teacher about expectations for classroom behavior. Rule setting and communication of expectations were discussed. He offered to help her establish a better climate once the semester was over. She stated that students should behave and it was not her job to have to be their parent. She retired at the end of the semester.

Example 2

An elementary classroom teacher was known to be a very solemn person who spent almost all of her time behind closed doors. If an administrator walked into her classroom he or she would have witnessed students in a third grade class with the heads in their hands, quiet but not engaged.

The teacher also was a crier. She did it behind closed doors. Students would tell their parents and parents would call the administrator. The students most likely were just concerned that this poor teacher was so sad. There were very few serious complaints about her teaching. She was able to "cover" the curriculum and stay focused on the established curriculum. It was just a very unhappy place.

The new administrator assigned to that elementary building spent time in the classroom and soon recognized that this teacher had a serious problem. She talked with the teacher and started a relationship with her to try to discover what her concerns were. As it turned out, this teacher was married to an alcoholic man who abused her.

In order to help this teacher, the administrator went with her to co-dependency meetings at the local hospital. They attended these sessions together for over a month and one day toward the middle of the year the teacher told the administrator that she was going to resign at the end of the year and move back home with her family, leaving her husband. This person became a real estate professional, made a great deal of money, and more importantly, became a happy person. She never fails to send a Christmas card to that principal every year.

Example 3

The head custodian in an elementary building was rarely seen outside the custodian office. He even had moved a recliner into that room. Witnesses stated that he was doing his personal laundry during work hours. He had poor working relations with the other custodians. One quit because of him.

The administrator started documenting and meeting with the head custodian over a period of three months, concentrating on expectations for the work environment and fulfillment of assigned duties. The progressive discipline plan continued to the point that the custodian needed to be dismissed. The dismissal was upheld by the Board of Education and surprisingly there was no request for any change in the decision from the man.

It turned out later that this person was a known pedophile, having served time in another state.

Example 4

"You will never amount to anything," and "You are an embarrassment to your parents." This teacher used those kinds of statements and much worse throughout her years of teaching. Students cried in her class; begged their parents to get out of that class; and conjured up all sorts of retributions against this high school teacher.

Parents wrote letters and stormed into that school on a regular basis, complaining about that teacher. The previous administrator had a hands-off attitude toward teaching and learning and concentrated on school management and activities. He would always suggest to the complaining parent that they should talk to the teacher, not him.

The new administrator wanted to change the situation. She started meeting with the teacher every time there was a complaint. It usually involved meeting with his union representative, as well. There were a great number of threats made by the teacher regarding her constitutional right of speech. The union representative actually started to try to help the teacher understand the damage that was being done to these students and offered to help the teacher change.

Once the union got behind the need for change, the teacher "saw the light" and tried very hard to monitor his statements. The teacher is still employed and the student and parent complaints have all but disappeared.

Example 5

Another case revolved around a teacher who refused to follow the district curriculum and was not receptive to any help offered. The teacher was not blatant about his refusal to use required curriculum but continued to use non-approved materials when not supervised.

The administrator worked on helping this teacher with individual staff development and focused his professional growth plan on the need to learn and use the district-required curriculum. The teacher tried to learn new strategies but would not sustain these efforts once the administrator edged back from constant observation and conferencing.

The administrator documented his behavior throughout two years and was about to make a recommendation to place this staff member on intensive assistance when this staff member made sexual overtones to a student. Parents made immediate complaints to the school and the police and the administrator moved to place him on administrative leave with pay while the case was investigated. While the case was being investigated the teacher decided to leave teaching and work in private industry.

Example 6

Another teacher was being moved from one building to another. She had worked in the other building for 32 years. There was little stated that was positive about this teacher. The receiving school administrator made an appointment to watch this teacher in her classroom prior to the move and then talked with her. The receiving administrator was very candid about the expectations at the new school. The teacher would be required to use technology even though she had never touched a computer and didn't want to. She would be required to keep parents informed and to work with staff in the instigation of new initiatives, all of which she had been reported as not doing in her previous 32 years.

The administrator spent a great deal of time in that classroom once the year started and offered continuous support through lead teachers and technical assistants. After three years of working for that administrator, the 35-year veteran decided to retire and start work as a consultant for a technology company. It has been stated that, "You can't teach an old dog new tricks," but this is offered as a case against that belief.

Example 7

Another custodian issue focused on failure to come to work. The absenteeism was documented and the documentation was shared and kept over a few months. This person was handed her separation letter and filed a request for a hearing. The hearing took place and the administrator and the district prevailed due to the complete documentation.

Example 8

Another incident of marginal staff focused on a tenured teacher who was not capable or willing to fulfill expectations for use of district curriculum strategies. This person chose to teach the way she had taught for ten years. She was vocal about not needing to change and not supporting the new research-based initiatives the district was asking staff to use to help teach reading. The administrator began work with this staff member and insisted that she use the approved strategies by continued support and observation. There was modeling of the strategies and more staff development offered. Many months of documentation ensued and the teacher was eventually placed on intensive assistance.

The process took another year but at the end of that second year, the teacher was dismissed. The subsequent hearing held in favor of the administrator and the district because there was substantial documentation and clear evidence that the teacher was offered many opportunities for help to improve but was unable or unwilling to do so.

Example 9

Another teacher was hired within a system that was just trying to fill a position due to consternation and reputation within a building. During the subsequent years that teacher had numerous complaints voiced against him and yet the administrator had not documented most of the complaints or actions.

When the new administrator was assigned to that building she was told she needed to concentrate on that person since so many students were being impacted and so many complaints had been voiced. After months of documentation of continued parent complaints, investigations into the complaints, and meetings with the teacher and their union representative, the teacher chose to find a job in a different district that did not ask for references.

Example 10

Another teacher was involved with students in what could be construed as an inappropriate manner, having them over to their house; eating dinner out with individual female students. This teacher was not married but had recently been divorced.

When a student mentioned that they enjoyed the teacher's attention their parents made complaint against the teacher to the school district administrators. The allegation was investigated and no immoral activity was found but the district asked the teacher to stop seeing students outside the regular school hours. The teacher immediately stopped and kept the administrators informed.

The pressure from the parents caused the teacher to decide to leave their position.

Example 11

A coach was alleged to be "dating" a student. When investigated, it was found that the coach was dating a graduated student. The district administrators talked with him about the impression he was making. He chose to move to a different district and eventually married that previous student. They have been married for 50 years.

Example 12

Finally, a teacher was accused of being belligerent, unprepared, and ineffective in the classroom. Even though the administrator worked in a highly unionized district, using persistence and continued documentation, as well as spending nearly a year in the hearing process, the teacher lost his job and the administrator went back to the building to continue to assure only good staff were working with his students.

Conclusion

Examples of marginal staff could go on for volumes, not just pages. An important theme throughout these examples is that there is a need for an administrator to assure that the employee is treated with dignity and respect. The staff member should be offered help to improve when appropriate. However, there are also times when the staff member should be dismissed due to the nature and circumstances of the behavior.

When working with marginal or incompetent staff a district needs to consider the systems they have in place for performance evaluation. The next chapter reviews supervision and evaluation procedures relating to performance.

PERFORMANCE EVALUATIONS

Importance and Purpose

Research shows that the quality of teaching in the classroom has a significant impact on student achievement. Therefore, It is essential that a well-designed evaluation system be in place so that good teaching can be promoted and supported in every school in the nation.

Along with the consistent procedures to be followed for review of all employees, it is important to assume that not everyone knows what their job responsibilities are. All employees need to be informed of expectations and their progress toward those expectations in a fair and clear manner.

A thorough, regular appraisal of teaching performance is also critical to the realization of the organization's goals. The primary goal of staff evaluations should be the growth of individuals, as well as the strengthening of the entire staff.

Formal appraisal based on individual organization's requirements should be conducted in an ongoing manner and should be required of all principals and supervisors. Even though there usually is a designated time frame such as a requirement of tenured staff appraisal every three years, it should be made known that appraisal and evaluation is not limited to that schedule but is a minimal requirement in supervising staff.

Continual evaluations should facilitate employee productivity and professional growth and encourage communication between staff and supervisors. Ongoing assessment should also document performance strengths and weaknesses and support disciplinary action or dismissal. Ultimately, continual evaluations should act to motivate and effect staff improvement and performance.

When the evaluation process leads to corrective action, the first goal should be to facilitate the employee's improvement rather than dismissal. There are a few incidents when that statement may not be true such as in cases that involve immoral, illegal or unethical behavior.

Every organization should have a system of performance appraisal. This system should include methods of progressive discipline and standards of documentation so that corrective action can be taken in a professional manner in times of great stress. Appraisal systems should adopt consistent standards on an ongoing basis so that unpleasant surprises are avoided.

Although some states have common forms for districts, most districts are required to create not only their appraisal systems but also their reports and forms as well. Some states are working to create common standards for effective or quality teaching. When devising a system, state efforts should be incorporated into the system including district forms. If there are stated standards in state law, they need to be included in the forms used within the district. Locally developed systems may need to be validated by the State Board. The selection and implementation of an effective evaluation system may be one of the most important decisions a school system can make. All steps need to be followed carefully and thoughtfully.

It should be expected in every district that the principals and supervisors exert every effort to encourage staff members to develop teaching performance to an optimum degree. Administrators should expect that they will neeed to devote a substantial amount of time and effort to accomplishing this task.

The appraisal system should be conducted in a fair and consistent manner and on a continual basis. Administrators should make every effort to understand the needs of the employee to be able to provide help toward improvement as needed. This attitude is of foremost importance in successful performance evaluation systems.

When a staff member's performance is unacceptable, the supervisor should specifically identify areas needing improvement and offer specific suggestions for improvement. The employee should also be given adequate time to show improvement.

All formal evaluations should be written and dated. The employee being evaluated should have time to review the evaluation with and without the evaluator. Both parties need to sign and date the appraisal statement. There also needs to be a channel for appeal of unfavorable appraisals.

If the employee's performance remains unsatisfactory despite the best efforts of the administrator, the employee should then be given a notice that non-renewal or dismissal is likely. All procedures should be followed and all deadlines met in accordance with state statutes, district policies and portions of negotiated agreements.

The district should expect timely evaluation and the employee should expect continuous efforts by the administration to assist them in improving their performance.

Districts and their administrators need to have systems in place to move toward dismissal if it is called for in the supervision plan. Moving people from one building to another or re-assigning administrators to start the process all over again is a way of avoiding what needs to take place. Most importantly, it is avoiding what needs to take place for the benefit of the students.

Evaluation Steps and System Examples

This section is offered to those organizations that may be considering the revision of their existing evaluation system or the creation of a new one. The following are some suggestions to consider. Throughout businesses and schools there are many systems that are based on the following.

There needs to be evaluation criteria that are usually directly derived from the job description and existing state standards for quality. Along with that, considerations should include proficiency in subject matter, ability to teach the required curriculum and perform assigned duties, alignment of employee's actions with the district and building goals, and in some districts, a review of pupil progress and growth.

Indicators for pupil performance might include authentic assessments, standardized test results, portfolio assessment, direct employee observation, and student work production. Other indicators might be disciplinary actions over time and student and parent climate surveys.

Other aspects of employee appraisal would include ability to work with others, record of attendance, punctuality and and ability to meet deadlines.

Preparation of Employee for Evaluation

Consideration should be given to the following when designing steps for orientation of an employee to the district's supervision and evaluation system:

- A review of the job description and corresponding expectations of the employee.
- A review of the district forms that are used for official evaluations.
- A review of the timeline for supervision and evaluation.
- A review of the expectations for probationary staff versus tenured staff.
- A review of the ultimate goal requirements in becoming a tenured staff or continuing employment.

Collection of Data

In order to make informed decisions on staff appraisals, it is important to gather data and then review that data based on pre-determined criteria. Data can be gathered in many ways and include the following:

- Direct observation of the employee in his or her assigned tasks and job-related duties.
- Notes or scripts of observations made by the supervisor.
- Samples of teacher or student work.
- Conferences with the staff member.
- Available indicators of student growth or job related targets.
- Previous performance reports.
- Climate surveys.

Annual Performance Review

Using the approved annual performance review document, the supervisor writes the review based on the pre-determined criteria using the observation data in the employee's working file. Some districts have this system on their web site and computer files while others use printed booklets and forms.

Once the report is prepared, a final performance review conference is scheduled with the employee and the supervisor. At that conference each section of the review should be discussed and the employee should be given time to respond to the report in writing. This official document needs to be signed and dated by both the employee and the supervisor and a copy is given to the employee for his / her record. A copy is kept in the working file of the supervisor and the original is usually sent to the district personnel office.

To encourage continuous supervision, some districts have a section that asks for a written plan for improvement or growth for everyone which is the starting point for supervision the following year. These plans often include areas of required growth, suggested methods for achieving that growth, and an expected timeline for implementation of the methods and specific responsibilities of the staff member and district for implementing the plan. The employee should be informed whether his / her performance is satisfactory and whether progress assistance or disciplinary action is recommended. In addition, there should be stated plans for indications of tenure status or progress toward that status.

Intensive Assistance or Disciplinary Systems

Every district needs to have a system that guides administrators through the steps of working with marginal or incompetent staff. Often, these forms follow the performance review of tenured staff in the official documents.

They often include a series of steps which is often called progressive discipline. An example might be on level one that an employee is informed of his / her unsatisfactory status and is given methods to work on improvement. Deadlines and checkpoints are often given at this level in order to assure sustained improvement.

Level two often moves a staff member to a more intense situation characterized by need to improve by a certain date to avoid consequences such as dismissal.

Level three involves district forms and procedures for disciplinary action and the steps that will be taken. The dismissial criteria, whenever possible, should be consistent.

It is highly recommended that a district set procedures to use when an administrator moves toward intensive assistance. Procedures should include the discussion of findings with the supervisor and / or director of human resources. Following the proper steps is crucial in this area. It is good to have more than one set of eyes review documents and data.

When dealing with the procedures involved with marginal or incompetent staff, a reminder is offered that the employee's ability to make a living at his / her chosen profession is on the line. Clear procedures and processes must be followed. There should be no question as to why the employee is at this step. Confidence in this step is determined by the quality and quantity of data that has been collected.

Since working with progressive discipline is extremely difficult, it bears repeating:

- Administrators are instructional leaders not social workers or punching bags.
- Insist on improvement and don't accept excuses.
- Be direct and clear in your expectations.
- Be consistent, treating like issues alike.
- Be consistent in record keeping for good and bad performance.
- Observe often and document, document, document.
- Deal with the facts, be honest and non-biased.
- Ask for help: Personnel, Attorney, and Assistant Superintendent.
- Do not destroy employee records without checking with legal counsel or human resources personnel.

Styles of Documentation Writing

The need to document has been repeatedly mentioned in this book. It is essential to have good quality writing and clear and concise directive styles. When writing memos and letters to marginal or incompetent staff, it might be helpful to consider using directive rather than passive writing. As work progresses with marginal or incompetent staff, it might be wise to consider the clarity and directness in speaking and writing. Examples follow:

Passive versus Directive Writing

Passive	Directive
1. It would be nice if you could get that in by next week.	1. This report needs to be in by 9:00 on Friday morning.
2. Would it be possible for you to stop yelling at students?	2. It is the expectation of this district, as stated in our core expectations, that all students will be treated with dignity. You are not to yell at students.
3. Have you the time to answer this by this evening?	3. Please return this to my office by 4:00 this evening.
4. It is nicer to not touch students in a rough manner.	4. Do not grab students again.
5. I don't like it when you grumble through our staff meetings.	5. If you have something to say about the staff meetings, either do it with me privately or ask for recognition by raising your hand and then you will be called upon for your comment.
6. It is better if you get to work on time.	6. It is an expectation of your job description to arrive at work fifteen minutes prior to work with students.
7. Staff members don't like you.	7. There have been five written complaints from other staff members about your unwillingness to perform your playground duties.
8. Can you take a shorter lunch break?	8. It is required that you take no more than a half hour lunch break.

Conclusion

Performance evaluation systems are critical to dealing with the marginal or incompetent staff member. Since performance appraisal systems will inevitably uncover instances of incompetence, it is incumbent upon the administrator to follow clear procedures that satisfy criteria related to due process and just cause. This is the important topic to which we now turn.

DUE PROCESS

Once an administrator has worked with an employee and is moving toward intensive assistance and possible dismissal, it may be of help to read through the following information regarding due process, just cause and looking at it from a union viewpoint.

In the Magna Carta, due process is referred to as the "law of the land" and "legal judgment of his peers." Some state constitutions continue to use this language. Due Process in the United States refers to how and why laws are enforced. It applies to all persons, citizen and alien.

There are two parts of Due Process, the "HOW" and the "WHY." Procedural Due Process, the "HOW," indicates that a law, policies, etc., must be fair, clear, and have a presumption of innocence to comply with procedural due process. The "WHY" is substantive due process. Even if a law or policy is passed it can be deemed unreasonable and that could make the law or policy unconstitutional.

Generally, due process guarantees the following, (although this list is not exhaustive):

- Right to a fair and public trial conducted in a competent manner.
- Right to be present at the trial.
- Right to an impartial jury.
- Right to be heard in one's own defense.

- Laws must be written so that a reasonable person can understand what criminal behavior is.

Just Cause

What is just cause? Simply put, it means the employer must have a reason for imposing discipline and the reason must be fair.

There are seven tests as to whether the employer has used "just cause" in discipline and discharge cases:

- Was the employee adequately warned of the consequences of his conduct?

    The warning can be given orally or in written form. An exception may be made for certain conduct, such as insubordination, coming to work under the influence of drugs or alcohol, stealing, or other immoral, unethical or illegal actions by the employee.

- Was the employer's rule or order reasonably related to efficient and safe operations?

    It may be a requirement in some positions that employees can require certain clothing to protect the employee but unless part of the contract, they cannot require certain colors of clothing.

- Did the administrator investigate before following through with the discipline?

The investigation is normally done prior to a decision to discipline is made. When immediate action is required, the best course of action is to suspend the employee pending the investigation with the understanding that he / she will be restored to his / her position and paid for time lost if he / she is found not guilty or the claim is unfounded.

- Was the investigation fair and objective?
    The administrator needs to be concerned about interviewing everyone present no matter what his / her position, such as both classified and licensed witnesses.

- Did the investigation produce substantial evidence or proof of guilt?
    It is not required that the evidence be preponderant, conclusive, or "beyond a reasonable doubt," except when alleged misconduct is of such a criminal or reprehensible nature as to stigmatize the employee and seriously impair his chances for future employment.

- Were the rules, orders, and penalties applied even-handedly and without discrimination?
    If enforcement has been lax in the past, administrators cannot suddenly reverse their course and begin to crack down without first warning the employees.

- Was the penalty reasonably related to the seriousness of the offense and the past employee record?
    If employee A's past record is significantly
    better than that of employee B, the employer
    may give employee A a lighter punishment
    than employee B for the same offense.

One of the main reasons why employees join unions is to gain protection. Contracts with employees should include statements such as the following: "Employees shall be disciplined or discharged only for just cause." Other phrases sometimes used are "proper cause" or "fair cause."

Employers must be ready to handle all sorts of discipline cases from warnings to suspensions to dismissals while adhering to just cause and due process.

Union Perspective

It may be an advantage to have some knowledge of how a union official may think when there comes a time to take part in a grievance meeting or a hearing. A union representative may think about the following when representing an employee in the organization:

- Did the employer meet the seven tests?
    Just because the employer did not follow all
    the seven tests does not mean they will lose
    but it helps the employee's case if the
    employer fails to follow all the tests.

- Try to stop the employer from suspending or firing the employee.

    Try to get a cooling off period. The case becomes harder once an employee is no longer working.

- Ask for all the employer's notes and records.

    All records, even personal notes of the administrator, are rightfully available to the employee.

- Do a thorough investigation of the case.

    Do not take the employer's statements as fact. Do a separate review of the case.

- In a grievance meeting make the employer prove their case first.

    It is important for the employee to have all the facts on the table. Justification is in the hands of the employer.

- There are two sides to every discipline case.

    Did the employee violate a known rule and what should the punishment be? The union will want to be sure that if proven that the employee did violate a rule or law and that the punishment fits the offense.

- If the employer refuses to back down from a written warning, union representatives usually make sure that the employer receives a written statement disputing the facts and the discipline. Insist that the letter is also put in the employee's personnel file.

Cautionary Information Regarding Unfair Dismissals

The legislation governing unfair dismissals does not protect the employee from dismissal, but it does provide a system of appeal where the fairness of the dismissal can be questioned. It is generally required that there is at least one year of continuous service by the employee for the employer to bring a claim, and the claim usually needs to be made within six months of the dismissal. It would be wise to check state laws regarding this issue.

It is the requirement of the employer to prove that the dismissal is fair if an appeal is made. If a judgement of unfair dismissal is found upon appeal, the employee can receive compensation for the loss of earnings caused by the dismissal and can often be placed back into his / her position.

The employee must have been working under a contract of service. There are exceptions and excluded categories in many state laws that prevent an employee of a stated category from bringing a claim. Again, it would be wise to refer to individual state laws on this issue.

The burden of proof to show that the dismissal was fair will be on the employer, not the dismissed employee. The employer can rely on capability-related issues, such as lateness, absenteeism, and persistent absence through illness. The longer the absence, the easier it is for the employer to show that it is causing genuine difficulty in terms of the organization's ability to be effective.

Lack of competence is another area that will show that the employee was unable to do his / her job. First of all, the employer must prove that the employee was made aware of the standards and expectations of the position. The employer must also be able to prove that improvements were necessary and that those were stated clearly to the employee. It should also be proven that the employer gave a reasonable time frame for improvement to occur. There should also be proof of a final warning to the employee of possible dismissal.

Qualifications for employment can cause a question about dismissal. If an employee misleads the employer about his / her license or work history when applying for the position, the dismissal can be upheld. Also, employee conduct is an area that when well documented will hold up on dismissal appeals. There is a need to distinguish between gross misconduct and ordinary instances of misconduct that continued for a period of time.

Redundancy is a reason for an employee to ask for an appeal on dismissal. The areas to watch out for are:

- That there was an economic justification for the reduction in force.
- That the position in question was not replaced.
- That there was a fair system used when reducing the workforce.
- That there was no discrimination used when choosing the personnel for reduction in workforce.

Although stated before, the reader is reminded that the following is required to assure that there is no unfair dismissal:

- To give appropriate warnings.
- To take adequate time to establish a case for dismissal.
- To allow the employee the right of representation.
- To assure that the dismissal process was followed according to the approved district process.

It also may be of help to review the following list of unfair reasons for dismissal:

- Employee took part in a strike when permitted by state law.
- Membership in a union or engaging in union activities off hours.
- Civil or criminal proceedings, actual, threatened or proposed against the employer.
- Race, color or sexual orientation of the employee.

- Age or membership in organizations.
- Pregnancy.
- Exercising rights under the Adoptive Leave or Parental Leave Acts.
- Unfair selection for redundancy.

Terms of Possible Interest

A **fixed-term contract** is a contract of a specific length and the length of the contract is known to both parties at the time of the signing.

A **specific purpose contract** is of a limited duration. Both parties know the length of the contract at the time of the signing.

Redress is given when a claim of unfair dismissal is upheld.

Reinstatement means the employee is treated like he / she was never dismissed. No loss of earnings from the date of dismissal is incurred by the employee and he / she is entitled to any increases in pay during the time he / she was not in their position.

Re-engagement means the employee gets his / her job back only from the particular date of the decision to re-instate. Often this means there is no entitlement to lost earnings.

Compensation is awarded at times when financial loss is proven. Injuries to feelings or stress caused by the dismissal are not usually valid claims for compensation.

As always, it is wise to review the state laws regarding the terms used in dismissal and the procedures used when an employee claims an unfair dismissal.

You are obviously interested in this topic or you wouldn't be reading so far into this book. So, if you are ready to start using some of what is offered here, consider two things as most important in efforts to work with marginal or incompetent staff:

Document, Document, Document!

There was a television show that used the following phrase:

"Just the facts, Ma'am."

When considering working with marginal or incompetent staff, keep in mind that the administrator needs to concentrate on facts and to document accurately and continually. The next section shares scenarios that have been fictionalized that could happen to an administrator when they tackle the task of dealing with marginal or incompetent staff.

As this section is read it needs to be stated that this is not a legal guide. It is always the responsibility of the administrator to know the specific state laws regarding personnel, the district policies and the contractual agreements between the district and personnel. What this book can do is help in the day-to-day issues that arise when working with staff who are not performing at an acceptable level.

Scenarios of Working With Marginal and Incompetent Staff

The following scenarios are offered to illustrate situations that an administrator may face when dealing with marginal or incompetent staff. These scenarios show behaviors and responses that the administrator may face. Being forewarned is being forearmed.

Scenario 1

Over a few months a new administrator to a building had made great efforts to get into every classroom everyday by walking through on a various times throughout the day and on a varied schedule. This principal had witnessed a particular secondary teacher who had yet to be anywhere but sitting behind his desk.

Students were behaved in that they were in seats, taking turns reading from the textbook, taking notes about a lecture or doing quizzes at their desk. The principal had never seen this style of teaching despite years of experience and extensive knowledge of teaching methods and styles.

Due to the fact that it was an expectation that teachers monitor student work and have genuine interaction with their students, the principal talked with the staff member in the hall in a causal manner. The principal remarked that he had noticed in his many visits to the classroom that the teacher had a style of teaching that included only whole group work and that the teacher always sat behind his desk.

The teacher stated that this is his preferred way of teaching, and he had been teaching that way for twenty years. The teacher stated that he felt that it is a successful way to have control in the classroom, and he stated that he hadn't had any complaints.

The principal stated that it is the expectation of the district that teachers vary their teaching style and cited the core expectations of the district. The principal then asked the teacher to try some different, more interactive strategies. The principal also offered staff learning opportunities to help the teacher become acquainted with the strategies. The teacher acknowledged the offer and then walked off to the teacher's lounge.

During the next few weeks, the principal continued his rounds and was unable to record a single time in which the teacher in question had changed any teaching strategy in his class-room. The students were still in rows and still doing the same things, as noted before.

The principal wrote a memo stating somewhat the same thing as was talked about in the hallway and stated that the teacher needed to sign it to indicate that he had received it. The teacher signed the memo but then returned to the same style of teaching.

After continued observations through visits to the classroom, the principal again wrote a memo stating that he would like to make an appointment to view the teacher's use of the required strategies. He stated that the observation needed to be scheduled within the next two weeks. That deadline passed.

The principal, again not seeing any changes in the teacher's classroom, wrote a letter that stated the teacher must comply with the directive to schedule an observation time to witness the use of required district strategies. The teacher then showed up to receive the letter with his union representative. The principal made a space for the union representative to sit but addressed his comments to the teacher stating that if he failed to make an appointment for an observation and failed to use the required strategies that a letter of reprimand will be placed in his district file. The teacher signed the letter to indicate that he had received it but stated that he did not agree with it and left the office.

The next week the teacher made an appointment to have the principal visit his classroom. The principal attended at the agreed upon time. The teacher used the same strategy as before, remaining rooted at his desk with students in rows. The principal wrote a response to the observation and shared that the teacher had failed to use the required strategies and that there was a staff learning session that the teacher could attend the following Tuesday that would help him become acquainted with the strategies.

The principal arranged for a substitute teacher so that the staff learning session could be attended by the teacher. The teacher came to that session but sat in the back and did not take part in the learning. The principal stopped by the teacher's classroom to talk about the staff learning session. The teacher said that it was worthless and that he learned nothing of value and did not intend to change his style of teaching.

The principal then stated that the teacher needed to be in his office at a particular time and that the teacher could bring representation if he wished. Before the meeting the principal prepared a letter stating the facts regarding the entire step-by-step process from the very first hallway conversation to the arrangement for staff development. The memo cited district approved curriculum documents that state that it is required to use interactive methods to teach students. The principal also communicated the fact that the teacher supervision and evaluation documents state the need for such use.

The teacher and his representative arrived on schedule. The principal shared copies of the letter and explained, step by step, the entire process. At the bottom of the letter it stated that if the teacher did not comply with the requirement to use interactive strategies that the teacher would be placed on intensive assistance. Also in the letter was one more offer for a staff learning opportunity. The teacher was also told specifically what compliance means and given a deadline to accept the offer. The teacher was also told that follow-up observation was required.

The teacher did not request the help of the staff-learning offer, and the deadline passed for another observation appointment. By then the teacher would not talk to the administrator and complained to others that he was being "picked on" by the administrator.

The principal followed appropriate procedures to place the staff member on intensive assistance and attached copies of the previous documentation to that document. To make a long story short, the teacher refused to change, the principal continued to follow the district procedures and eventually the teacher's contract was not renewed.

The teacher took this through the proper channels of appeal. The outcome of the hearing was that the teacher is no longer working in that district.

Well, it may seem like a lot of detail work by the principal, but in the long run when that administrator now walks into that room there is a teacher who has students engaged in learning who have smiles on their faces instead of their heads in their hands.

Scenario 2

In this second scenario a teacher associate is reported to be having an affair with a high school boy in her neighborhood. This was reported to the principal by one of the staff members who is credible and who had actually witnessed the reported behavior. What should the principal do?

This principal encouraged the teacher who reported it to her to also report it to the authorities, which she did. The authorities pursued an investigation, and eventually found enough evidence existed to substantiate the accusation. This associate was arrested.

It became public knowledge since it was reported in the newspaper. The principal recommended placing the associate on unpaid leave until the case was finalized. The district upheld that recommendation.

The principal documented each step and kept it in a working file within the building. The final recommendation to the district to place the employee on leave without pay was the only piece of documentation that was placed in her district file.

The employee eventually resigned her position and was found guilty of the inappropriate affection toward a minor.

Scenario 3

One staff member was a very friendly person who liked to talk to people and did so, on a regular basis about individual students. Although there were many rumors of this concern brought to the attention of the administrator there was never any specific example shared until a discussion was overheard at a business party when the teacher was having a general discussion about how students are coming to the schools less and less prepared to learn. She gave examples of behavior and then moved into examples using specific names of students.

An accounting of the incident was shared by another staff member who happened to overhear the comments and found them to be inappropriate and possibly a breach of confidentiality. The administrator took copious notes during the conversation and then talked with the teacher in question. The teacher denied having said anything inappropriate. The principal gave a verbal explanation and warning that it would a breach of confidentiality if that did happen. The teacher assured her that the discussion was not necessary.

A few months passed and the administrator overheard that above mentioned teacher talking at a staff development session about specific students in her class who had special education individual education plans. The administrator asked the teacher to come into her office where she gave the teacher a memo explaining the situation and also included a directive to never have a repeat of this type of discussion about individual students.

Scenario 4

Over the past few years there had been numerous discussions in this particular school teacher's lounge on all the expectations that were being placed upon teachers regarding achievement. Many teachers voiced their opinions and were vehemently opposed to only being concerned about test scores.

Although the discussions were often lively, the majority of the staff understood that due to public opinion and the State and Federal requirements, there really wasn't any choice.

They preferred addressing the concern and showing that they could be held accountable even though they felt the measure wasn't appropriate.

Staff development sessions were offered on data analysis and strong curriculum strategies to help the staff improve their teaching, which would then, ultimately, improve the test scores.

One teacher felt so strongly that she would not be held responsible for test scores that she refused to take part in the staff development sessions and continued to instigate conversation with other staff to try to get others to refuse the staff development.

The principal called the teacher to her office to talk about her concerns. She recognized the teacher's beliefs and stated that even though she has a right to her opinion she preferred that the teacher not continue to instigate dissention regarding test score accountability. The teacher sat in the office and just stared at the principal. At the end of the conversation, the teacher got up and walked out.

There was no change in the teacher's behavior and the principal sent a written memo delineating the conversation that was held and stated that she wished the teacher could change her mind and help the school move the test scores in the proper direction. The teacher wrote a note on the bottom of the memo stating she didn't believe in it and would not participate.

The principal left the issue alone for a month and then wrote another memo stating that the teacher really needed to comply and offered to help her understand any of the staff development she had missed. The teacher just ignored the memo.

Again the principal left the issue alone and by now the time for the norm-referenced tests was looming. The principal wrote a note asking that the teacher talk with her students about the importance of the tests to encourage them to do their best on the assessment. The teacher wrote a note on the bottom of the memo stating that she would not comply due to her belief system regarding test score accountability.

During the days of the testing, the principal walked through the building and found this particular teacher sitting at her desk while the students took the test. No monitoring of the test was evident throughout the testing days in this teacher's class.

When the test results came back, that particular teacher's class scored many points below the other classes in that grade level.

What was the problem with scenario? The principal was not explicit enough in her expectations and she did not escalate the documentation to the required level so that the teacher understood that there would be no exceptions. It is important to be consistent, clear and concise in directing marginal staff.

Scenario 5

Another scenario involved a teacher who had been teaching for over ten years in one particular school. Although having taught many grade levels, the teacher had never taught anywhere else in his career.

When reviewing the working personnel file left by previous principals, the new administrator noticed numerous pieces of documentation showing parental complaints about this teacher either with specific incidents or by demanding that their children not be placed in that class.

The new administrator decided to try to do something about this the very first month of his tenure in that building. He met with the teacher and shared the concerns as noted in the file with him and stated that there was a need to improve relations with the families. He asked the teacher if he had any ideas to share at that time and offered resources to read that might start some thinking in that area.

The teacher asked to check out some books and discussed some of the findings with the principal. The administrator started spending more time in the classroom and every time there was a parent complaint, that complaint was shared with the teacher.

After a few weeks it became apparent that the anger parents showed toward that teacher had to do with the way the teacher stated things. The teacher was scattered in his thinking and often used inaccurate words. He also talked in circles.

If a specific statement were taken out of context, it could easily be misinterpreted or interpreted negatively.

The administrator discovered that the teacher wasn't purposefully being negative toward students but was merely incompetent in his communication skills. With full intent to help this teacher, the administrator started going into the class in order to script the teacher and give feedback to him. When they sat together there was a genuine agreement that there was intent to help. The teacher paid attention and tried to incorporate the suggestions for improvement.

This effort, along with video taping the class, went on for over a semester. Unfortunately the complaints from parents continued and the efforts the teacher made to communicate with the parents ended in more negative feelings toward the teacher.

After many months of continued attempts to help this teacher, the principal candidly asked if the teacher had thought of retirement since he was eligible. The teacher decided to think about it and at the end of the school year retired. The union representative was never brought in. The teacher left to pursue other endeavors. A ten-year problem was brought to a congenial ending for the teacher, parents and principal.

Scenario 6

It is hard to believe but in this next scenario a teacher who had been asked to come into the office to discuss her refusal to contact an angry parent came to the meeting with a hidden microphone and tape recorder.

The teacher had numerous complaints voiced against her due to the fact that she is considered a cruel person to the children in her fourth grade class. Parents had reported disparaging comments, grabbing of student work and tossing it in the garbage can, and her unwillingness to even talk to the parents about these reported incidents.

The meeting was called by the principal to share the most recent complaint. The purpose of the meeting was to give the teacher the official letter that was to be placed in her file regarding a clear statement that no disparaging remarks will be allowed in her classroom. This letter included a record of the many discussions and memos that had been previously shared with the teacher.

The principal asked the teacher to sit down at the table with her so they could go over the letter together. The teacher pulled the chair very close to the principal and said, "Are you going to give me one of those nasty memos again? I am getting very tired of our conversations." The administrator explained that the meeting was called due to the fact that another parent complaint had been voiced and she proceeded to explain the details of the complaint and the subsequent investigation. Four students who were independently interviewed corroborated that the event happened as stated by the parent. The principal had documented all of those interviews.

The teacher stated that the letter was not necessary and that the "Kids just make up stories and get their parents upset." The principal referred back to the letter and explained each section, one at a time, stopping to ask if the teacher needed to have any part of the letter explained, especially the section dealing with the ramifications. If one more complaint were received, the teacher would be to be placed on intensive assistance. The teacher ripped up the paper in front of the principal and said she would not sign it.

The principal then printed off another copy of the letter and stated that the teacher's signature indicates only that she has received the letter and not necessarily that she agreed to the contents. The teacher, in an angry tone, stated she would not sign it. The principal then asked her secretary to come into the office to witness the teacher's refusal to sign the paper and to witness that the teacher had received her copy of the letter.

The secretary left after signing the letter at the bottom that she had witnessed the teacher receiving the letter.

At that point the teacher pulled out the hidden tape recorder and pushed it into the face of the principal, who merely stated that she has the right to have a tape recorder as long as one person in the conversation knows about it. The administrator then closed the meeting.

Eventually, the teacher was placed on intensive assistance. Her hostility and refusal to deal with the concerns lead to dismissal, which was supported in a hearing due to the immense stack of documentation that was provided by the administrator.

Scenario 7

A principal of an elementary school was having a leisurely Sunday morning with his coffee and paper when he read the headline, "Local Teacher Arrested for Heroin Use." That caught his attention but after a more thorough review of the story his stomach became knotted. In the story it stated where the teacher worked, what grade level and, of course, the teacher's name. The article described in great detail that he had worked with elementary students for five years at XYZ School whose principal was, guess who?

After the paper hit the floor, the phone started to ring. Parents called, staff called and a hoard of media were not only on the phone but some had stationed themselves outside his door.

He was having various reactions including denial since he hired this teacher who was excellent in the classroom and a favorite among staff and parents. He thought to himself, don't forget all those extra hours the teacher had given to the drama department. He then went on to think that if he wanted all this media attention he might have decided to stay in that band he played in during school that hit the front page of the paper. But since this negative issue hit the paper instead of his lost accolades, he was expected to handle this situation.

After getting dressed and sneaking out to the car through the attached garage, he got away from the house quickly. A media truck had already arrived out front of his home. He headed for the school and his office where he had all the district policies and all his files. He again snuck into the gym door in the back of the building since there were media personnel by the front door.

Once in the school he headed for his office through the dark corridors. The office door was then shut behind him. Grabbing the school district policies, he hunted for anything to do with drug use or illegal use or felonies. He found the policy on staff convictions of a crime. Hmmm, well the teacher has not been convicted but had been arrested.

The next step was to call his supervisor and then the Director of Personnel to discuss options with them. According to the district policies and the union contract, it was considered too disruptive to keep an employee on the job when an issue such as this had happened, so it was decided to recommend that the employee be placed on administrative leave with pay until the investigation was complete.

The principal drafted the letter and e-mailed it to the Director of Personnel. Waiting for the phone call back, the principal took deep breaths to calm his nerves. The call came and the letter was approved. The employee, out on bail, was informed via the telephone that a substitute teacher would be hired for his classroom until all of this was straightened out. The employee was extremely upset and denied all charges.

After leaving his office the principal headed for home. The media were still waiting to pounce on the principal outside his home but he merely stated to them that it was inappropriate to comment without more knowledge about the alleged drug arrest. The principal got back into his house and spent the day in turmoil.

To shorten the scenario – the teacher was eventually found to have been set up and that his roommate was the one with the drug concern. It was the roommate who had left the paraphernalia in the teacher's car which was found when he had been stopped for speeding.

The teacher was exonerated of the charges and reinstated in his classroom. Always be certain that staff are treated with dignity and don't assume complaints are accurate until proven so.

Scenario 8

The issue of staff stealing from other staff members is a situation that causes a deep feeling of violation from the staff, especially when the accused staff member is well liked and very personable.

A teacher came to the office of the principal and stated that she was missing a fifty dollar bill from her purse. The purse had been in a desk drawer. The administrator asked the staff member if there was any chance that she had used the money or if someone in her family had taken the cash. She was assured that this wasn't the case. The staff member was totally devastated because she needed that money for a particular expense right after work.

A week later another staff member reported that she thought someone was stealing money from desk drawers. Her pop fund was depleted. That staff member's comments were documented as well as the first complaint, including the dates and times that she talked with the principal. The approximate amounts taken were also documented.

Throughout the next few weeks more people suggested that coats and money had been stolen. All incidents were documented and by now the principal was seriously concerned. When money is taken out of one's purse or wallet, one often thinks that one was mistaken regarding the amount that was originally there. It just isn't expected that someone would paw through personal belongings and steal money.

The principal rented a covert camera and set up a situation in a teachers' lounge where a purse was fairly easily accessible. In the purse was some bait money. The camera was left on for a couple days. The purse was checked every half day or so to see if anything was missing. On the second day the principal discovered that the money had been stolen and the tape was on. The administrator retrieved the tape and searched for evidence. Bingo! There it was right in the middle of the day. An employee was caught on tape reaching into the purse, taking out the wallet and then stealing the money.

The administrator called the police who sent over a detective who confronted the employee. The principal also called the head of personnel to inform them of the situation. The thief denied everything until the officer shared the videotape. Upon seeing the video, the thief admitted to stealing most of the things that had been reported missing. The person was charged and released on her own recognizance. The principal met with the employee and escorted her to her work area to retrieve personal belongings. The employee was told that she was on administrative leave without pay and that person could call personnel with any questions.

The employee was then escorted from the building.

A few weeks later the former employee went to court where they were found guilty. A victims report was filled out before the sentencing a few weeks later. Everyone who lost money or items included their concerns in the report. The documentation gathered after every reported incident came in handy in completing the paperwork.

Restitution was required of the former employee by the judge and the former employee was given a long time to pay it off. The ex-employee did not question her release from employment.

Conclusion

This chapter shows the importance of taking systematic steps to ensure that standards of due process and just cause are adhered to. It is important to recognize that actions taken by the administrator that result in dismissal or termination can be the subject of appeal. It is incumbent upon the administrator to prove the case and document that all procedures and criteria have been met. An important element of this is evidence and documentation of all communications with the staff member that have taken place. Supervision and communication are discussed in greater detail in the following chapter.

SUPERVISION AND COMMUNICATION

When supervising, evaluating and reporting on employee behaviors, remember that there are two basic principles to follow: due process and just cause (both of which were previously explained). Union grievances and costly litigation do not need to a part of the process if all the steps are completed properly. A great resource who may be of help when considering supervision of staff and communication would be Mary Jo McGrath who has written extensively about these issues based on the following.

When approaching an employee with a concern, the administrator always needs to be prepared ahead of time. A first time discussion should be as clear as written documentation. If time allows, consider practicing the meeting with a supervisor or someone from personnel.

It is essential that all communication, whether oral or written, be kept in strictest confidence. Make arrangements to talk where the conversation will not be overheard.

Always follow state laws, local policies and any union contracts that affect the district.

Administrators should not be in this alone. Be certain to contact the personnel department and your direct supervisor when dealing with marginal or incompetent employees.

Supervision

Always keep staff informed of any expectations, as well as
any new or revised rules. It is best to do this in a written
form such as a handbook. This permanent directive can
then be used as reference if an employee chooses not to or
is unable to follow directives. The date that the documentation
is provided to the employee should also be noted. This can
be done in a letter or as part of an agenda for a meeting.

As an instructional leader, there will be times when a
legitimate, work-related incident or pattern of behavior in
an employee must be handled. The steps below are used
universally but were cited from the Iowa Association of
School Boards suggestions. The following is offered to help
correct employee behavior and keep the district from
grievances and employment litigation as an administrator
works through personnel concerns:

1. Who was involved?
   - Cite the name of the employee.
   - Cite objective evidence, including witnesses.

2. What rule was violated?
   - If specific, cite it.
   - If not specific (poor judgment, unpro-
     fessional behavior), identify district
     standards and objectively state how the
     behavior noted failed to meet acceptable
     standards.

3. Where and when did the violation occur?
   - Cite objectively with no opinions or speculation.

4. Knowledge of rules
   - Cite when and where the rule was communicated to the employee.
   - If available, attach a signed copy of the rules acknowledgement form.

5. Rule violation history
   - Attach previous memos or letters or an explanation of a previous discussion.
   - Note any previous assistance the employee might have received for a violation.
   - Note any work-related importance of the rule, (positive work environment and legal requirements).

6. Impose discipline
   - Cite action that will be taken.
   - Cite why this step is a clear link between discipline and the work-related rule.

7. Authority statement
   - Be certain the administrator's supervisor knows about this action.
   - Cite district, State or Federal authority related to the rule.

8. Documentation
   - Obtain employee's signature that states he /
     she received the document.
   - If he / she refuses to sign, note the refusal
     to sign while employee is present and then
     make copy for him / her.
   - Reflect on any employee discipline in all
     annual forms, such as a summative report.

Communication

It is important for an administrator to write and speak clearly,
as well as objectively, when documentating employee behavior. The following is a guideline for written communication:

Use Facts Only

1. Use timely communication and narrow the focus
   to one item if possible, per memo or letter.

2. Be focused, clear and specific.

3. Use only the facts (Who, What, Where, When).

4. Refer to a published authority, such as district
   policies, state law, code, a handbook, district
   curriculum or specific dated prior directives.

Measure The Impact

1. State how the behavior affects students, staff, community, administration and others.

2. Convey observations from others: comments from co-workers, parents, students, etc.

3. Remind them of employee training that he / she has been offered or participated in that relates to the issue.

4. Read back to the employee specific comments made by him / her reflecting their attitude.

Relate Prior Intervention

1. Remind the employee if other offers had been made to help.

2. Remediate his / her concerns.

3. State what efforts have specifically been made to correct concerns. Be specific if no discernable effort has been made.

4. Indicate if there has been a pattern of similar behavior.

5. Attach previous documentation.

Action Needed For Remediation

1. Be clear and concise as to what the employee must do in order to be at an acceptable level of performance.

2. Offer resources that may help the employee improve.

3. Specific measurements should be used to show grow or lack thereof.

4. Schedule a follow-up meeting within three weeks.

Opportunity for Response

1. Always provide an opportunity for the employee to respond.

2. Be sure the employee knows what he / she is responding to and that he / she has had time to read the document.

Fairness In Record Keeping

1. The employee must be informed that documentation exists and is being retained (cc: file).

2. The employee must be informed that he / she has the right to comment in writing and to have

the comment included with the original documentation.

3. Informing the employee of the concern needs to be done in a timely manner. A good test would be if it were done early enough to allow the employee to gather information from his / her own perspective.

Documentation and Filing Conclusion

1. Any materials that may have an effect on the employment of an individual must be available to that individual.

2. The material must not include anything gathered prior to the employment of that individual.

3. Every document should indicate that the employee had an opportunity to respond and that response, if written, should be attached to the original document.

4. Keep in a working file, separate from the official personnel file.

Discipline Needs to Be Progressive

There needs to be an increasing formality of language when communicating with an employee on concerns over time. The continuum might be defined as follows:

- Talk – communication using the four aspects: facts, impact, prior intervention and action needed.
- Memorandum – written communication using some of the above elements.
- Letter – written communication using all of the above elements plus ramifications.

Another easy way to remember this might be:

- Verbal reminder
- Written reminder
- Written reminder with warning of termination

A **Progressive Communications Schematic** that follows might offer more clarification:

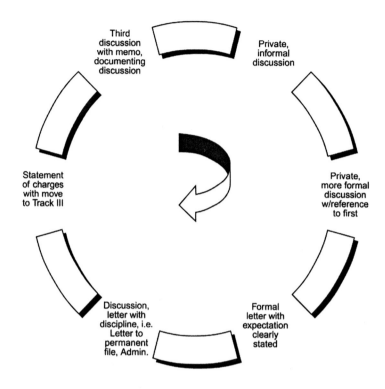

Third discussion with memo, documenting discussion

Private, informal discussion

Statement of charges with move to Track III

Private, more formal discussion w/reference to first

Discussion, letter with discipline, i.e. Letter to permanent file, Admin.

Formal letter with expectation clearly stated

The schematic shows that actions should be taken in a progressive fashion with increasing formality of communication and disciplinary intervention. Marginal employees may respond more quickly to progressive escalations and achieve "average" performance through intervention. However, the administator should be aware of the possibility of recidivism if continual supervision is not taken. Incompetent employees may require the complete cyle of progressive escalation depending upon the nature of the incompetence.

Often administrators need to work with employees who are insubordinate. Insubordinate means the employee does not subject himself / herself to the authority of the administrator or recognize the administrator's authority. In some cases insubordination such as employee refusal to do his / her job is cause for immediate discipline, unless the order by the administrator is determined to be illegal, immoral or unethical.

What would dealing with insubordination look like on a schematic? The following might be of help in explaining the process:

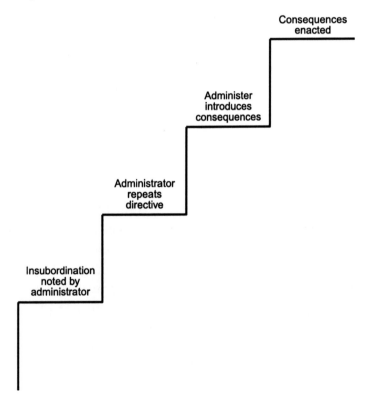

Consequences
enacted

Administer
introduces
consequences

Administrator
repeats
directive

Insubordination
noted by
administrator

There are times when immediate dismissal is appropriate. Standards for immediate dismissal are generally set by state statute. The most common bases for dismissal are the following:

- Immoral conduct.
- Dishonesty.
- Violation or refusal to follow district policies.
- Conviction of a felony.

The schematic for such an offense would be as follows:

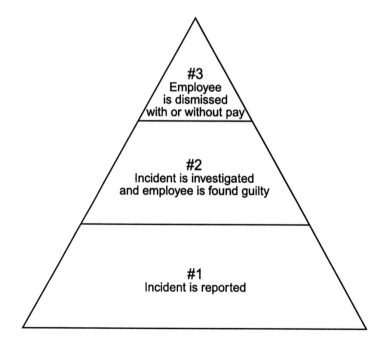

#3
Employee
is dismissed
with or without pay

#2
Incident is investigated
and employee is found guilty

#1
Incident is reported

Conclusion

Educators are very valuable. Even though many administrators have heard from wary staff that they may be "out to get" teachers, it is unlikely that any administrator would want to dismiss an employee without cause.

Hiring staff is a time-consuming task. Administrators want their staff to be of high quality so that the goals for the school and district are met. In the accountability climate that public educators find themselves, it is essential that excellent teachers be in every classroom.

Administrators face enormous tasks and do not wish to take on more activities than are necessary to successfully manage their schools and districts. The amount of paperwork associated with the management of marginal or incompetent staff is daunting, at best. There are very few public school administrators who are looking for more to do with the limited time they have.

Good teachers do not want to teach next to poor teachers. They may support staff as educators, but those who are really proud of their profession do not want examples of poor quality teaching or service tainting their reputation or making their work harder.

When administrators deal with marginal or incompetent staff they may not receive accolades from their staffs, but beneath the surface they are more respected. Most importantly, they benefit the children who need them.

In the next section, a detailed case study example of the progressive escalation model is presented. This includes step-by-step examples of memos, letters, forms, and actions.

COMPREHENSIVE CASE STUDY EXAMPLE

Throughout this book there has been a great deal of information offered that may be of help when working with marginal or incompetent staff. The following section is a complete case study that shows steps, memos, letters, forms, actions and final documents concentrating on one teacher.

Hopefully, reading and working through the documents will be helpful in the creation of similar documents when working with staff in progressive disciplinary manner.

The scenario that has been chosen is one that most principals will experience at some time during their career. The situation would, hopefully, not escalate to the level that is depicted in this case, but the entire progressive discipline process is shared.

In the education field there are staff members who feel and act like they are doing students a favor to be in their classroom and that any disciplinary concern is not their fault but that of the students. There are teachers who choose not to learn and grow but to be stagnant. In this scenario there is a teacher who is very unkind to students on a regular basis. She is marginal in her ability to teach according to goals and her behavior is one of insolence.

The teacher in question had been in this particular school for 15 years and had a history of parent and student complaints. A series of principals had been assigned to this building over the years due to the fact that it is a smaller building where many of the new administrators started their career but then moved into a building or position with more responsibility.

On becoming the administrator in this building, Ima Principal, the new principal, has been at her assignment for only a few weeks. She is working in her office before the teachers have returned. On one particular day she has a very angry parent come into her office to state that he did not want a particular teacher to be his child's teacher. He demanded that his child be moved to another teacher's classroom.

Ima Principal asks the parent to state in writing his complaint. The angry parent complies with the request. That complaint is as follows:

August 13, XXXX

Dear Mrs. Principal:

I am writing to request that my child, Bobby, not be placed in Mrs. Norapport's class. I prefer having Ms. Efficient for my child this year.

The reason why I do not want my child in Mrs. Norapport's class is that last year she yelled at my neighbor's child and my neighbor had trouble all year with that teacher. I do not want to go through the same thing she did. My child does not have to be in a class like that.

If my child is not moved from that class, I will be calling the school board.

Mr. Will Demand

Once Mrs. Principal received the above complaint she made a copy to discuss with Mrs. Norapport once she came back to school after summer vacation. She prepared and sent this memo to Mrs. Norapport:

Memorandum – Anyschool USA

TO: Mrs. Norapport
FROM: Mrs. Principal
DATE: August 18, XXXX
RE: Parent Complaint

Message Area: Yesterday, I received a written complaint from a parent that I will be sharing with you on August 23, XXXX at 2:00 p.m., (after our staff meeting). If you come in early to school and would like to discuss this before that date, stop by or call my office to set up an appointment.

Employee Reply:

Mrs. Norapport	*Ima Principal*
Employee	Administrator
Date:	Date: August 18, XXXX

While she was waiting for Mrs. Norapport to stop by and for the entire staff to come back after summer vacation, Mrs. Principal decided to go through the employee working files within the principal's office. She also reviewed the student management software files. As she looked through the files she used the following matrix to keep track of any particular concerns with the teachers assigned to Anyschool:

Chart Summarizing
Concerns in Personnel Files

Completed by Mrs. Principal 8/19/XX
Files reviewed were from the last ten years.

Staff Member	Parent Complaints	Weaknesses Noted on Observations	Absenteeism	Discipline Referrals
Teacher A	3	2	14	12
Teacher B	1	1	2	6
Teacher C	0	0	0	0
Teacher D	0	0	5	0
Teacher E	0	1	18	5
Teacher F	4	0	22	10
Teacher G	6	4	0	13
Teacher H	3	2	0	15
Teacher I	2	1	2	7
Mrs. Norapport	28	14	48	142
Teacher K	6	12	2	32
Teacher L	2	0	1	12
Teacher M	0	0	10	0
Teacher N	0	0	15	19

During the analysis of the above table, Mrs. Principal noticed that Mrs. Norapport had significant concerns in all of the areas, with the exception of absenteeism. Forty-eight days absent in ten years averages less than five days per year, and she found that Mrs. Norapport had undergone surgery one year that caused her to be gone for two weeks. Although she had the largest number of days absent, her record was for the full ten years whereas most of the other staff members had not been there for the full ten years.

One other teacher, Mrs. K, also had significant concerns and Mrs. Principal made a record to consider placing her on the observation track for the upcoming year. She also placed Mrs. Norapport on the observation track of the supervision plan for this year. A memo was prepared that was to be handed to all staff as to who was "on-cycle" versus those who are not for the upcoming year.

The memo was divided into four parts: first, the new teachers to the district who were on the first track and who did not have standard licenses; secondly, the tenured teachers who were "on-cycle" and who were going to be observed this year; third, the teachers who would be on observation for next year and the third year teachers who would be scheduled for observation. At the bottom of the memo it stated that principals could adjust the schedule as they needed to and would inform staff members of their status for observation per district policy at the beginning of each school year.

The week before the year was to officially start, Mrs. Norapport stopped by to meet the new principal. Mrs. Principal invited her in and offered her coffee. They talked for a while and then Mrs. Principal shared the above memo on the parent complaint from Mr. Demand with Mrs. Norapport. Mrs. Principal explained that it is her policy to let any professional staff member know if there is a complaint. Mrs. Norapport was offered a chance to respond. The following is how she responded:

Memorandum – Anyschool USA

TO: Mrs. Norapport
FROM: Mrs. Principal
DATE: August 18, XXXX
RE: Parent Complaint

Message Area: Yesterday, I received a written complaint from a parent that I will be sharing with you on August 23, XXXX at 2:00 p.m. (After our staff meeting.) If you come in early and would like to discuss this before that date, stop by or call to set up an appointment.

Employee Reply: I don't agree with Mr. Demand and I don't appreciate it if you don't stand up for your staff. In the future I hope you will just tell parents to talk with the teachers and leave you out of it like the other principal.

I will take his son off my roster and put him on the other fifth grade class roster, which will make that class larger, but I guess you can handle that issue.

Mrs. Norapport	*Ima Principal*
Employee	Administrator
Date: August 20, XXXX	Date: August 18, XXXX

Mrs. Norapport signed the memo and the original was placed in the working personnel file for her in Mrs. Principal's office. Mrs. Principal made a point of talking with her about her statement, trying to reassure her that it was her policy for all professional staff to inform them of any complaints. She mentioned the review of all the staff's personnel files and stated that there were many parent complaints noted in her file. If there were some in the future, those would be handled in the same way as it was for Mr. Demand. Mrs. Norapport didn't say anything but just looked at Mrs. Principal.

Meanwhile, Mrs. Principal was working very hard to get everything prepared for her first meeting with her new staff. She thought it might be a good idea to have proof that she handed out the important handbooks, so she created the following memo to be attached to those documents and to be given out at the first staff meeting:

Memo – Anyschool USA
Mrs. Ima Principal, Administrator Ima Principal
August 22, XXXX

To: Anyschool Staff

Attached you will find materials of great importance to you as you start you school year here at Anyschool USA. Please read each of the booklets that are attached to be assured that you have all the information you need to perform your duties in this school.

As always, I offer my help in any way that might be needed to better understand the rules, regulations and expectations. For those who are new to our school this year, please meet with me to discuss these on August 24, XXXX at 1:00 p.m.

Attached you will find the following booklets:

• The Building Information Handbook
• The Approved Curriculum, (As appropriate to your grade level)
• The Supervision and Evaluation Handbook

Beyond that, state statute books relating to education can be found in the professional library, along with the district policy book.

Every professional educator is responsible for all school procedures, district policies and procedures, State and Federal law. Again, if you find a need to have further discussion on any of these, don't hesitate to make an appointment with me to discuss them.

Have a wonderful year!

The staff meeting went well and the year started without too many concerns. There were four more parental complaints against Mrs. Norapport. One on October 20 and one on October 23rd charged that Mrs. Norapport treats girls better than boys. Another parental concern came on Nov. 1, XXXX, regarding gender bias from a parent who was also an educator in another building in the district. Each was handled in exactly the same way as the first. Mrs. Norapport gave up responding to them and just signed the memos without comment. The original copies of the signed memos went into Mrs. Principal's working personnel file for Mrs. Norapport, and a copy went to Mrs. Norapport.

Mrs. Principal asked that all staff who were on the observation cycle this year make appointments with her to start the observations. In October she had observed all except Mrs. Norapport. She had asked her many times to schedule the observation, but she hadn't. Finally, Mrs. Principal took her calendar down to Mrs. Norapport's room and scheduled the first observation. Mrs. Principal asked Mrs. Norapport about what she would witness in the observation and what would help Mrs. Norapport in the way of feedback. Mrs. Norapport stated that she would have to think about that and get back to Mrs. Principal. The observation objective came via e-mail the day of the observation.

The following is the report of that first observation:

Anyschool USA
Mrs. Ima Principal,
Administrator

October 23 XXXX

TO: Mrs. Norapport
RE: Teaching to the Approved Curriculum

Observation Objectives: "To show how dinosaurs are still very important to the world around us."

Observation Notes:

This classroom observation was held on October 22, XXXX, at 2:00 p.m. Your classroom was set up so that all students were facing forward in the classroom in their individual desks. You had the word "Dinosaurs" written on the white board and there were various dinosaur drawings hung around the front of the classroom.

2:00 – 2:08
You were standing in front of the class as the students put their reading books away. You had asked them to get out their science books and their notebooks and pencils. As the students were getting their materials ready, various students were talked to directly by you: "Marta, you still don't have a sharpened pencil?" "Randy, who gave you

permission to go to the pencil sharpener?"; "I do not have time to listen to that concern."; "What does that have to do with dinosaurs?"

You reminded the students to hurry up and get their things out at 2:05. At 2:07 you said that you were going to count to ten and at ten you expected all students to be facing forward and quietly sitting in their seats.

2:08
You started the lesson by stating that dinosaurs are still very important to our lives. We can learn a lot from the fact that they were big and dangerous and that they had few predators. You also stated that, "They can teach us about being too arrogant because you never know what is about to hit you in life." You stated that the dinosaurs disappeared but they really don't know why that happened. Then you went into describing the various types of dinosaurs depicted in the drawings around the room. Students interrupted you on occasion to ask questions about whether there are any dinosaurs left, what happened to them and why they all died. You continued to describe the types of dinosaurs. You spelled the names so the students could write them in their notebooks. Two students wanted to know if some were meat eaters or plant eaters and you said that wasn't what you were talking about at this time. Another student said that he had all of this in second grade. You said he was being rude.

2:22
You asked the students to draw a picture by the name that they wrote in their notebook of the dinosaurs so they could remember what they looked like. You gave them thirty minutes to do this.

As the students did their drawings, you sat at your desk reading the science book.

3:00
You asked the students to put their notebooks away and get out their free reading books. They were told to read until it was time to clean up for the end of the day.

Observation Questions:

- Where in the approved curriculum for fifth grade is the study of dinosaurs?
- How is it that you chose this topic for this class?
- Considering the dinosaur topic, what was your main objective for this lesson?
- If it is to indicate their importance, how was the assignment of the drawing meeting that objective?
- How do you know if your students know more about the importance of dinosaurs than they did before this class?
- Other reflections from this lesson?

Conference Overview: At our meeting relating to the lesson on dinosaurs, you shared your thoughts regarding reflection on the above questions. You stated that dinosaurs are especially interesting to students and you have some very nice materials that you have collected over the years. You said you chose to teach it as a special lesson even though it is not part of the approved science curriculum in fifth grade.

When discussing your objective you stated that you really wanted them to be able to recognize the various kinds of dinosaurs, not whether they are important to our society any longer. I mentioned that you had stated to me what your objective for this lesson was in our pre-conference. You made mention that you decided to change it but did not tell me before the observation.

You were asked if you intended to follow the curriculum in future lessons and you stated that you do. You were asked to set another observation within two weeks so that could be observed. You said that you didn't think that was necessary since you had just said you were intending to use the curriculum. It was then stated that it is an expectation. Another observation is now set for October 30, XXXX.

You were challenged to be sure that you were using the approved science curriculum and that you had a specific objective for that lesson that would be conveyed prior to the observation. You were also offered an opportunity to discuss the fifth grade curriculum with the science facilitator, which you declined, stating it wasn't necessary.

Opportunity for Response:

Mrs. Norapport   *Ima Principal*
Mrs. Norapport   Mrs. Ima Principal
DATE: October 23, XXXX   DATE: October 23, XXXX

It should be noted that Mrs. Norapport did not have anything to add to this observation report under her space for employee response, but she did sign it.

Soon after the first formal observation, Mrs. Principal was walking through the building during a regular instructional day when she overheard Mrs. Norapport in her classroom. Mrs. Norapport was talking with three boys in the front of the class with a raised voice.

The following is the documentation that Mrs. Principal added to her personnel file for Mrs. Norapport:

TO: Mrs. Norapport
FROM: Mrs. Principal Ima Principal
DATE: Nov. 1, XXXX
RE: Informal Observation

Today at 9:30 a.m. while I was doing my walk through of our building, I stopped outside your classroom door when I heard you speaking in a loud voice. I stepped into the back of the room to witness you stating the following: "All of you boys will never make anything of yourselves. How embarrassing for your families that you have no drive. I guess I was wrong to assume you would do your work when asked to do so."

The boys were standing there trying to move so they didn't face the class, one of them was in tears. As you moved toward them, one of them moved back away from you.

You then looked up and saw me standing in the back of the room. You then stated, "All right, you boys can sit down now."

This is an example of the concerns that have been noted by students and parents for a number of years. You and I discussed your numerous complaints at the beginning of the year and you were told that all students will be treated with dignity and respect as stated in the core expectations found in the Supervision and Evaluation Handbook which you received the first staff meeting of the year and were told officially that you are responsible for all contents of all the handbooks.

You are directed to not use disparaging remarks to students, and if they need to be corrected you will do it in private in a supportive manner. I am offering you the opportunity to check out some books from my personal collection on disciplining with dignity. If you choose to use that resource then we will make an appointment to discuss the book or books once you have had time to read it.

To be perfectly clear, you are to no longer use any belittling remarks to students. Any reports or complaints could result in disciplinary action.

Response Opportunity:

Mrs. Norapport
Mrs. Norapport
Date: November 1, XXXX

Mrs. Principal asked that Mrs. Norapport meet with her right after school on November 1, XXXX. Mrs. Norapport arrived and sat at the table as invited to by Mrs. Principal. She sat facing the wall and made no comment as Mrs. Principal explained the memo and the directive. When asked if she would like to make a response, she wrote the following, signed the memo and roughly slid it across the table toward Mrs. Principal. That response follows:

TO: Mrs. Norapport
FROM: Mrs. Principal Ima Principal
DATE: Nov. 1, XXXX
RE: Informal Observation

Today at 9:30 a.m. while I was doing my walk through of our building I stopped outside your classroom door when I heard you speaking in a loud voice. I stepped into the back of the room to witness you stating the following: "All of you boys will never make anything of yourselves. How embarrassing for your families that you have no drive. I guess I was wrong to assume you would do your work when asked to do so."

The boys were standing there trying to move so they didn't face the class, one of them was in tears. As you moved toward them, one of them moved back away from you.

You then looked up and saw me standing in the back of the room. You then stated, "All right, you boys can sit down now."

This is an example of the concerns that have been noted by students and parents for a number of years. You and I discussed your numerous complaints at the beginning of the year. You were told that all students would be treated with dignity and respect as stated in the core expectation, which can be found in the Supervision and Evaluation Handbook. That handbook was received by you at the first staff meeting of the year and was told officially that you are responsible for all contents of all the handbooks.

You are directed to not use disparaging remarks to students, and if they need to be corrected you will do it in private in a supportive manner. I am offering you the opportunity to check out some books from my personal collection on disciplining with dignity. If you choose to use that resource then we will make an appointment to discuss the book or books once you have had time to read them.

To be perfectly clear, you are to no longer use any belittling remarks to students. Any reports or complaints could result in disciplinary action.

Response Opportunity: **I saw you slinking around this morning and fully expected that you were going to do something like this. Students need to be disciplined or our classes would be in total disarray. I was merely telling them that they needed to get their act together.**

Mrs. Norapport

Mrs. Norapport
Date: Nov.1, XXXX
cc: file

Mrs. Principal placed the signed copy of the memo into the working personnel file of Mrs. Norapport.

It wasn't long that the following concern was brought before Mrs. Principal. The other fifth grade teacher, Mrs. C, came to the principal's office and stated that she was worried about what was happening in Mrs. Norapport's classroom. Being new to the building she wasn't sure how to handle this concern. Mrs. Principal asked her if she would put her concern in writing, and Mrs. C said she would. The following was the memo written by Mrs. C:

Nov. 10, XXXX

Mrs. Principal:

I feel I need to share what I sense is going on in Mrs. Norapport's classroom. My room is right across the hall from hers and I hear her raise her voice to students on a frequent basis. She yells at them. I think she also has a tendency to yell at the boys more than the girls.

The reason I wrote this memo is that I worry about how this is affecting those students.

Mrs. C

Mrs. Principal thanked Mrs. C for her memo and stated that she could not discuss personnel issues with her but that she appreciated her caring and concern for the students. The memo was added to the personnel file in Mrs. Principal's office regarding Mrs. Norapport.

It started with one staff complaint and then members of the staff started coming by to tell Mrs. Principal of other concerns. Mrs. Principal asked that each document his / her concerns, but only a few wanted to make "an official complaint."

Mrs. Principal decided that the concerns needed to be documented so she used the following table to keep track of the concerns and the dates they were voiced by staff members:

Staff Concerns Regarding Mrs. Norapport since November, XXXX

Staff Member	Date	Concern
Mrs. C	Nov. 10	See attached memo.
Mrs. D	Nov. 12	Noted student crying as they were going out to recess from Mrs. N's classroom.
Mr. G	Nov. 14	Stated that N was short with him as he pointed out she was talking too loud in her classroom – sounded like yelling.
Ms. I	Nov. 17	Stopped by Mrs. N's classroom to find out why none of the boys had come to art. Mrs. N was holding all the boys in her classroom for discipline.
Ms. E	Nov. 21	She stated that kids had told her in her class that Mrs. N was very mean and wasn't there anyone who could help them?
Mrs. C	Dec. 5	She still is concerned about the students and wanted to know what was happening.
Mr. N	Dec. 14	Wanted to know that he had talked w/ Mrs. N for ten years and didn't like the fact that she was being picked on by a new administrator.
Mrs. L	Dec.23	Told Mrs. C who stated that Mrs. N refused to let her boys in her class participate in the Xmas pageant. The girls were allowed to practice most days.

The example of the above table grew as the year progressed. She kept track of comments made by staff and attached written memos such as below when the staff member agreed to put his / her concern in writing. The following are memos from teachers who wrote out their concerns:

Nov. 20, XXXX
Mrs. Principal:

I think something should be done about how unfair Mrs. N is treating the boys in her classroom. The girls get to go to the pageant but the boys do not. There isn't any reason that should be allowed in our school.

Mrs. C

Dec 23, XXXX

Mrs. Principal

I saw three boys crying in Mrs. N's classroom today and she wouldn't let me in to try to help. She actually yelled at me. What are you going to do about this?

Mr. G

Mrs. Principal remained consistent on how she handled every complaint she received on any teacher. She always shared whatever she could with the teacher, treating them like a professional. No information on Mrs. Norapport was given to any person complaining except appreciation for their caring for students. She continued to do that with Mrs. Norapport. The following is a memo that is an example of the system for informing staff members of complaints and this was given to her about the continued staff complaints directed at her:

November 15, XXXX

Mrs. Norapport:

In the last four days I have received three complaints, one of which is formal and is attached, regarding your behavior, as witnessed by fellow staff members. All three were concerned about how you treat students.

As we have discussed before and specifically in the Nov. 1, XXXX letter I gave to you, under no circumstances are you to treat students in an undignified or belittling manner. I stated in that letter that if further incidents were to occur, then disciplinary actions could be imposed.

Since this has happened, as stated by other teachers, you will have this letter of reprimand filed with the Director of Personnel, in your permanent file.

You have been heard and seen belittling students, specifically the boys in your class. Students have been seen crying; teachers and myself have heard you using a loud voice with students and treating boys and girls differently within your class.

Under no circumstances will you be allowed to continue using these actions with your students. If there are any more incidents of this nature, then the ramifications could include recommendation for Intensive Assistance Level A.

You are specifically directed to see me at 4:00 p.m. this afternoon in my office for a discussion about ways to help you overcome these concerns and to be certain that any questions you have are answered. Failure to attend this meeting will result in placement in Level A, Intensive Assistance.

Employee Response Opportunity:

Mrs. Norapport   *Ima Principal*

Mrs. Norapport   Mrs. Principal
Nov. 15, XXXX   Nov. 15, XXXX

Mrs. Norapport attended the meeting at 4:00. She had a union representative with her. Mrs. Principal welcomed the union representative, but Mrs. Principal directed her comments only to Mrs. Norapport, only answering questions from the union representative.

Mrs. Norapport stated that she had been teaching for many years and had never had any complaints. Mrs. Principal then took out Mrs. Norapport working personnel file and shared the information that was researched about the past ten years and stated that she had, in fact, had numerous complaints.

Mrs. Principal also stated that she was working with Mrs. Norapport based on witnesses, complaints and observations made within this year. The other complaints and concerns were in the file, but she was not basing her decision on possible Intensive Assistance on anyone else's reports.

Mrs. Principal then went on to say that Mrs. Norapport was scheduled to go to a workshop for two days focused on classroom management. Mrs. Norapport was directed to attend the workshop and write a plan on how she was going to implement her new learning. The plan was to be due Friday, Nov. 17, XXXX, by 4:00 p.m.

Mrs. Norapport took the letter after asking to re-read it and have time to respond. Mrs. Principal stated that her response and the signed letter were due back in her office by noon tomorrow.

The letter was returned by 9:00 a.m. and on it Mrs. Norapport stated that she didn't care to attend any more in-services and that she did not see a need for them. She stated to Mrs. Principal that she did not need a substitute for those two days.

 Due to Mrs. Norapport's refusal to take part in the workshop, Mrs. Principal wrote the following letter:

Mrs. Ima Principal
Anyschool, USA 00006

Mrs. Norapport
Fifth Grade Teacher
Anyschool, USA 00006

DATE: December 19, XXXX
RE: Intensive Assistance

This letter is to officially inform you that you will be recommended for Intensive Assistance starting in January of XXXX. As you know, over this year I have been observing your class, sharing written documentation, copies of which are attached. You also have had numerous complaints that have been shared since August XXXX. Copies of those are also attached. You have received all of these reports.

Due to the fact that numerous opportunities have been offered to you for growth and change, the next step is to officially place you on Track III, Intensive Assistance.

I have set an appointment for you on Wednesday, Dec. 20, XXXX, here in my office at 8:00 a.m., which is when most staff will be at an inservice in another building. At that time I will explain in detail any questions you might have regarding this step. I have attached a copy of the district's intensive assistance program for your review prior to the meeting.

If Wednesday, Dec. 20, is a problem for you, see me for another time, but it must be completed before Friday, Dec. 22, at 9:00 a.m.

Sincerely,

Ima Principal
Mrs. Principal

Employee Response:

Attachments
cc: file

Although Mrs. Principal had kept her supervisor informed about these concerns throughout her efforts to work with Mrs. Norapport, she made an appointment with her so that this letter could be reviewed and she could practice the meeting with her supervisor before she talked with Mrs. Norapport. The letter was then given to Mrs. Norapport.

Her supervisor looked through all of the documentation and approved the placement of Mrs. Norapport on Intensive Assistance, Level A. They then discussed the possible scenarios that could happen with an employee when placed on the third level of supervision. Mrs. Principal left with belief that she could handle the conference but was feeling very uneasy about it.

Mrs. Norapport came at the appointed time for her meeting with her union representative. The Union representative tried to dominate the conversation, but Mrs. Principal smiled at her and stated that she appreciated their effort to represent their member, but that this meeting was going to be directed at Mrs. Norapport.

Mrs. Principal went through the letter and the district level three, Intensive Assistance, Level A, step-by-step with Mrs. Norapport. Basically, level A states that it is the teacher's responsibility to understand how she needs to improve and that offers for assistance will be available to the employee if she chooses to take advantage of those offers. The teacher will continue to be observed as before and any complaints will be shared so that Mrs. Norapport knows how she is progressing.

Mrs. Norapport was very quiet in the meeting, asking only if she was being fired. Mrs. Principal explained the process and that the purpose was to officially offer assistance. She asked Mrs. Norapport if she could state back to her what she just said. Mrs. Norapport stated that she was being given the opportunity to improve and all improvements would be noted, as well as any complaints. Mrs. Principal agreed that was the situation.

She then went on to say that if improvements were not noted then she would possibly be placed on Intensive Assistance, Level B, which includes the offer of an outside team of professionals observing her and giving feedback. She has the right to accept or decline that offer if she were to be placed on that level.

Mrs. Norapport signed the letter without comment and the two ladies left Mrs. Principal's office. Mrs. Principal watched as they left and then sat at her desk and tried to calm herself down. She was actually shaking.

Even though Mrs. Norapport was placed on Intensive Assistance, Mrs. Principal continued with the formal observations of all the teachers who were on-cycle, and it came time to set up another formal observation of Mrs. Norapport. She had followed through with the observation of another science class where Mrs. Norapport used the required curriculum and taught as a whole group.

Mrs. Principal had followed the same system for observing the class during the second time and added a comment that follows regarding use of district curriculum: "Mrs. Norapport, during this specific lesson, you taught directly from the district approved curriculum. You did not use the district strategies for hands-on science. You have participated in three years of workshops and the district science facilitator has worked with our fifth grade team to assure that you know the strategies. Please review the attached science strategy description as noted in the approved science curriculum handbook." Mrs. Principal went on to schedule a planning meeting session with the science facilitator for the next week. Mrs. Norapport attended that session.

Moving forward on observation requirements, Mrs. Principal then asked Mrs. Norapport to choose a lesson focusing on the use of the new reading strategies. Mrs. Norapport had taken part in four days of teacher training on the use of these strategies. There had been continuous discussion at the staff meetings to extend that knowledge and to have the staff share their learning as they used the strategies. It was going very well for most staff members. Mrs. Norapport was one of the few who felt strongly that she didn't need to change how she taught reading and was verbally against the strategies in the staff meetings.

The date was chosen for the observation and the objective for the observation was given to Mrs. Principal the night before the observation. The report is as follows:

TO: Mrs. Norapport
FROM: Mrs. Principal
DATE: November 28, XXXX
RE: Third Observation

Observation Objective: To show proficiency in the use of the new reading materials. (Mrs. Norapport's objective.)

To show proficiency in the use of the new reading imitative strategies with students. (Mrs. Principal's added objective.)

Observation Notes:

9:00
Your classroom was set up in rows with students facing forward. There was a folding table in the back of the room that was leaning against the wall. The new reading materials were piled along the counter on the south side of the room.

You asked the students in the front of each row to go get enough books for each row and hand them out. The students did that and all had their books by 9:03.

You held up the book and you said you were going to talk about the book before you asked them to read it silently. "The front cover of the book has a picture of a tree and grass. What else do you see in the picture?" One student raised their hand and said that there was a flower by the tree. You agreed that there was a flower, but you asked them for more significant items. Another male student stated that there was a tent and you confirmed that by stating that it certainly was obvious enough.

You pointed out the title and then you opened the book to the inside and showed the title again and showed the class where they could see the information about the author.

You asked them what they thought the book was about and one boy stated that it was probably about camping. You said that they should now read it silently to find out what the book was about. You gave them a half hour to do that.

As the students read you walked to the back of the room and then back to the front of the room and then sat at your desk. You kept your eyes on the students as they read.

The students started finishing the short book by 9:15 and you told them to re-read the book to be able to answer questions about the story. Some of the students did this while others flipped through the pages or sat at their desks without doing anything.

At 9:30 the class was asked to put their books down and you said, "Was the book about camping?" A girl offered that it was and you said she was right. You then asked what other things could they say about the book and a few students offered their thoughts. At 9:38 you asked them to put their books on their desk so that the first one in the row could pick them up. You asked them to get out their spelling book to look at the next lesson while they were waiting to go to art.

At 9:45 you instructed the students to line up for art class and then you escorted them to that class.

Conference Questions:

- Your objective for this lesson was to show proficiency in the use of the new reading materials. Please share how you felt you did in the use of the materials.
- I added an objective and that focused on the new reading strategies that all staff have been trained to use and are expected to use in their reading classes. Share examples of how you implemented the strategies you learned in your sessions.
- What new knowledge did the student gain from this lesson?
- Knowing your directive to treat students with dignity and respect, pick out examples of how you did that in this class.
- How have you used the strategy to work with students in groups?
- Other reflections from this lesson?

Conference Overview: Mrs. Norapport, your observation was on your use of the new reading strategies as have been taught to you over the last year. One of the strategies is to move from whole group to working with smaller grouping so students with like abilities can learn from one another. You have the table that was bought for your room but you have not used it yet.

You do have the materials and have them ready for use with the class but you are still teaching in whole group. Before our next observation, please see the reading strategist for assistance in your class to help you set up groups. She will schedule time to model for you how to do the reading strategies and work with you as you start using them. I will schedule another formal observation in December so it is expected that you will work with the reading strategist as early as the end of this week so you can show proficiency in the use of the strategies.

Response Opportunity:

Mrs. Norapport   _Ima Principal_
Mrs. Norapport   Mrs. Principal
DATE: November 2, XXXX   DATE: November 2, XXXX

Mrs. Norapport chose to not respond to the observation and merely signed it and gave it back to Mrs. Norapport. Mrs. Principal called the reading strategist to schedule a time for her to work with Mrs. Norapport and she sent Mrs. Norapport the following memo regarding this plan:

November 2, XXXX

TO: Mrs. Norapport
FROM: Mrs. Principal
RE: Reading Strategist

As discussed in our conference relating to your third observation in your reading class today, I have called Ms. X, the district reading strategist, who will be coming to spend Monday, Wednesday and Friday with you next week.

The schedule will be as follows:

Monday – The first day she will model the required reading strategies with your class during your regularly scheduled reading class. You are to send to her the book you would be using for that class by tomorrow evening.

Monday – during your planning time, you will work with Ms. X to discuss the strategies used and to have your questions answered so that you can plan with her your lesson for Tuesday and Wednesday.

Tuesday – you will use the district strategies with your students as planned with Ms. X.

Wednesday – you will teach the district reading strategies with Ms. X assisting as a team teacher.

Wednesday – during your planning time you will make the necessary arrangements to continue with the required district strategies for Thursday and Friday.

Thursday – you will use the district strategies by yourself with your class.

Friday – Ms. X will observe you using the district strategies as planned on Wednesday and she will make observational notes.

Friday – during planning, you, Ms. X and I will sit down to discuss your progress in the use of district reading strategies.

If you have any questions about the schedule. Please see me this afternoon before you leave for the day.

Ima Principal
Mrs. Principal

Ms. X, Mrs. Norapport and Mrs. Principal sat down to discuss the week's efforts in the use of the district reading strategies. Mrs. Norapport stated that she didn't like the strategies and felt that her previous style of teaching was fine for all the students she had before.

Ms. X reported that during both Monday and Wednesday, she taught the class because Mrs. Norapport chose to sit in the back of the room. They planned together but by the questions the students had, the plans were not followed on Tuesday and Thursday. She stated that on Friday, Mrs. Norapport had used a whole group method of teaching. No effort was expended toward use of grouping during that reading class.

Mrs. Norapport stated again that she didn't use the district strategies and she had no intention of using them.

The following memo, documenting the above was given to Mrs. Norapport at 4:00 on Friday:

November 9, XXXX

TO: Mrs. Norapport
FROM: Mrs. Principal
RE: Reading Strategist Plan

As discussed in our conference relating to your third observation in your reading class, I called Ms. X, the district reading strategist, who agreed to change her schedule to spend Monday, Wednesday and Friday with you this week.

The schedule was as follows:

Monday - The first day she was to model the required reading strategies with your class during your regularly scheduled reading class. You were to send to her the book you would be using for that class by the end of the next day.

Monday – during your planning time you worked with Ms. X to discuss the strategies used and to have your questions answered so that you could plan with her your lesson for Tuesday and Wednesday.

Tuesday – you were to use the district strategies with your students as planned with Ms. X.

Wednesday – you were to teach the district reading strategies with Ms. X assisting as a team teacher.

Wednesday – during your planning time you were to make the necessary arrangements to continue with the required district strategies for Thursday and Friday.

Thursday – you were to use the district strategies by yourself with your class.

Friday – Ms. X was to observe you using the district strategies as planned on Wednesday and she was to make observational notes.

Friday – during planning, you, Ms. X and I sat down to discuss your progress in the use of district reading strategies.

Ms. X, you and I met to discuss the week's efforts in the use of the district reading strategies. You stated that you didn't like the strategies and felt that your previous style of teaching was fine for all the students you have had before.

Ms. X reported that during both Monday and Wednesday, she taught the class because you chose to sit in the back of the room. You planned together but by the questions the students had, the plans were not followed on Tuesday and Thursday. She stated that on Friday, you had used a whole group method of teaching. No effort was expended toward use of grouping during that reading class.

After hearing Ms. X's report, you stated again that you didn't use the district strategies and you had no intention of using them.

Mrs. Norapport, as stated in the district curriculum handbook, page 18, paragraph three, "All elementary teachers are to use the approved reading strategies as stated below...." You choose not to use them.

You have participated in all the required training offered by the district and you have had extra help by the district reading strategist, as described above. You still state that you will not use the reading strategies as required.

Due to the fact that you are unwilling to use the required district reading strategies, a copy of this letter will be placed in your permanent file at the district office.

You are directed, officially, by me to start using the district reading strategies in your classes as of Monday, November 11, XXXX. I will stop by your class once per day during the next week to observe your use of the strategies.

Ima Principal
Mrs. Principal

Employee Response: **I do not intend to use the district strategies because they do not work any better than the style of teaching I have been using for years.**

Mrs. Norapport
Mrs. Norapport

Cc: file

Mrs. Norapport was given the opportunity to read the letter over the weekend but she chose to write the above response that Friday evening and gave the letter back to Mrs. Principal as she walked out the door. Mrs. Principal made a copy of the letter, placed it in a sealed envelope and left it in her desk until Monday morning when she delivered it to Mrs. Norapport in her classroom.

Mrs. Principal stopped by each day during reading to witness the change in Mrs. Norapport's style of teaching reading. On the same day of the observation the following incident happened as was documented by Mrs. Principal in the following manner:

November 16, XXXX

TO: Mrs. Norapport
FROM: Mrs. Principal
RE: Report on Reading Strategy Use

As stated in the attached letter, you were directed to use the required reading strategies and I was going to stop by each day for a week to witness your use of the strategies. Throughout each reading lesson, for the entire five days, you continued to use only whole group and there was no evidence of any use of grouping of students or any of the required reading strategies.

Please find the attached official letter requiring you to use the strategies. If you have anything further to discuss regarding this directive please indicate in the following response section.

Ima Principal
Mrs. Principal

Employee Response:

Cc: file

No response was given to this memo and it was included in the growing number of artifacts in Mrs. Norapport's working file within the principal's office.

Another incident happened on November 3, XXXX, which dealt with Class Climate and the requirement that Mrs. Norapport was given to treat all students with dignity and respect. The following is the letter that explains that incident:

Mrs. Ima Principal
Anyschool USA
0010 School Street
Whoknowswhere, Ia 50000

Mrs. Gottsa Norapport
Fifth Grade Teacher
Anyschool USA

November 3, XXXX

RE: Class Climate

The purpose of this communication is to focus on your relationship with students in your class and to provide you with current techniques for increasing a harmonious class climate.

Four boys from your class (Brad M., Scott O., Dan L., and Craig Z.) came to talk with me on Thursday, November 2, XXXX, during their lunchtime. After speaking separately with each of them, the following incident was conveyed as having happened yesterday.

On Wednesday, November 1, XXXX, it was reported that you told the students in your classroom that you had been keeping track of those students who were handing in homework. You told the class that the girls had all turned in all homework while only six of the thirteen boys had turned in all of theirs. You told the class that, "Girls are smarter than boys, so it doesn't surprise me that the girls were better at following directions and caring about their work." You then went on to tell them that, "All of the girls could take part in a popcorn party, but none of the boys would be able to go." When the boys that had turned in their homework asked why they couldn't go, you said, "If you want to participate next time, get the boys to hand in their homework."

As noted in the attached memo I sent to you on October 20, XXXX, we talked about class climate once in September and twice in October when you lined students up and compared them academically by gender. I directed in that memo that you cease segregating students by gender. On October 23, XXXX, I witnessed your class walking to the gym in segregated lines. This is in violation of my directive to you on October 20, XXXX.

Title IX of Federal Law specifically prohibits discrimination based on gender. Anyschool USA District Policy clearly states in 143.9 that no gender discrimination will be tolerated.

You are considered biased when you deal with students differently based on gender. Such behavior is counter to the district's expectation for class climate. Due to your continued behavior, the parents have been complaining. This jeopardizes the confidence that the majority of our district's teachers and administrators have earned.

Three parents have written formal complaints of which you have copies. Mrs. Myson has commented in her letter dated November 1, XXXX, that her son has no desire to compete in class because he feels boys have no chance to excel in your classroom. Mr. Childmine is adamantly opposed to having his daughter taught in an environment based on gender bias. Mr. Girlsonlygreat feels that he will be demanding that his son be taken out of your class due to lack of academic expectation for his success.

After the first staff meeting of this year you, along with the entire staff, were given the opportunity to attend the increasing positive class climate seminar.

You stated in our meeting on September 10, XXXX that you feel that teaching by rewards based on gender creates more competition. When it was pointed out that your comment and beliefs are contrary to the class climate seminar and the expectations based on district policy, you stated that you would try to change your methods.

Due to the fact that we have had numerous conversations since you stated that you would try and that there is little indication that you have tried to change, for the next three weeks you are to have your detailed lesson plans on my desk by 12:00 noon each Friday for the following week. In those lesson plans there needs to be obvious and clear directions as to how you are going to change from teaching with bias to teaching within the polices of the district and within Federal Law. This is to start the day after tomorrow and will continue for three Fridays. I will be observing your class throughout these three weeks with the express purpose to see your use of alternative strategies to eliminate gender bias.

We will next meet on November 8, XXXX, at 2:00 during your planning time to review your progress.

This letter will be kept here in your working personnel file, and you are welcome to attach a response to this document.

For the benefit of your students, you are expected to implement a successful plan that will be continually sustained.

Sincerely,

Ima Principal
Mrs. Ima Principal

Cc: Principal's employee file

Response Opportunity: Mrs. Norapport refused to sign this letter. *Ima Principal*

Nov., 3, XXX
Cc: file

Mrs. Norapport stated to Mrs. Principal that she had never been treated so badly by any previous administrator; she refused to sign the letter and just handed it back to Mrs. Principal. Mrs. Principal made a note in front of Mrs. Norapport that she had been offered an opportunity to respond and had been given a copy of the letter. The note also stated that Mrs. Norapport refused to sign the letter. Mrs. Principal signed and dated the note.

During the entire semester, Mrs. Norapport continued sending students down to the office for disciplinary reasons. Many of the issues were concerns with students not having the proper materials ready, escalating to students "mouthing off" to Mrs. Norapport.

Parent complaints continued from demands to take their children out of Mrs. Norapport's class to concerns about how a particular child was having trouble sleeping and refusing to go to school. In total to this point, there were eight more complaints from parents.

As an administrator gets further into the progressive discipline process it might be wise to review a few helpful phrases.

When writing memos or letters use clear direction phrases such as the following:

- Please do the following by...
- I insist that you...
- You are directed to...
- Have your students do the following...
- Return the following to me by...
- Have this done by...

Do not use:
- Would you mind responding to...
- Perhaps you would...
- You may wish to...
- Why don't you...

Examples of Informational Phrases (used for conveyance of factual information):

- Board Policy requires that all staff...
- A satisfactory evaluation will require the following...
- Regulations state that...

Continuing with Mrs. Norapport and Mrs. Principal...

Since Mrs. Principal was seeing little effort by Mrs. Norapport to change, she decided to review the personnel file she had regarding Mrs. Norapport and organize it in some fashion. She continued by using an adapted version of her original form:

Staff Member	Parent Complaints Since August 13, XXXX	Weaknesses noted on Observations during XXXX	Memos and Letters Written Regarding Concerns During XXXX	Student Discipline Referrals During XXXX
Mrs. Norapport				

In review of the above table that organizes the concerns regarding Mrs. Norapport, what would the reader do next?

_____   At the next concern write a letter with a sterner tone.

_____   Recommend Mrs. Norapport stay placed on Intensive Assistance Level A

_____   Recommend Mrs. Norapport be placed on Intensive Assistance Level B

_____   Talk to the your supervisor to consider recommending non-renewal of her contract at the end of the year

_____   Other?

Mrs. Principal decided to recommend that Mrs. Norapport be placed on Intensive Assistance Level B. Her reasoning for that was that Mrs. Norapport had been a tenured teacher in the district for many years and this was her first year as a principal in that building. It seemed prudent to use the entire Intensive Assistance district plan prior to making any recommendations for non-renewal.

There are some who would argue that Mrs. Norapport was being insubordinate and that this insubordination is grounds for immediate dismissal. They would recommend that route. Discretion, in a situation like this, would be the responsibility of the principal on advice from her supervisor.

Moving forward in this scenario...Mrs. Principal has decided to recommend Intensive Assistance Level B for Mrs. Norapport. What would be the reasons for the recommendation? Would she concentrate on teaching to the district curriculum with required strategies or use the gender bias concerns that had been so vehemently voiced in the last few months? Would it be possible to use both? After a quick review of the memos and letters, she decided to use both.

As she gathered her organized file and made copies of all documentation, she made an appointment with her supervisor and the district lawyer to discuss the letter that would be written and the process to follow as an employee is placed on the last level of the employee supervision and evaluation model.

The table that organized the number of complaints came in very handy as she explained her reasoning to use both issues in the rationale for placing Mrs. Norapport on the most extreme level. When meeting with her supervisor and the district lawyer, they reviewed the documentation, drafted the letter that follows and role-played the meeting when Mrs. Principal would give Mrs. Norapport the official word about Intensive Assistance Level B.

TO: Mrs. Norapport
FROM: Mrs. Ima Principal
 Administrator, Anyschool USA
DATE: December 20, XXXX

RE: Recommendation for Intensive Assistance Level B

Throughout this year you have received numerous discussion, memos, and letters from me regarding concerns from parents, students, teachers and observations made by me. You have made it very clear in your response that you do not see a need to change your behavior. I have attached the documentation regarding these issues.

Due to the fact that up until now you have not changed your behavior as addressed in the attached memos and letters, I am recommending you for Intensive Assistance Level B to commence in January XXXX.

The difference between Level A Intensive Assistance, where you are now, to Level B Intensive Assistance is that you are officially offered support from a team of people assigned by the Assistant Superintendent who will observe your work with students and give you feedback. There will be no written documents or oral reports given to the Assistant Superintendent or myself other than when the team has completed their work with you.

You have the opportunity to accept or deny this offer for guidance. You must make the decision by January 4, XXXX, in writing to me. If you choose to avail yourself of this support, the team will be assigned and start working with you by the middle of January.

There will be no change in the supervision and evaluation process as this team works with you. I will continue to observe you and give written feedback and any and all complaints will be documented as they have been throughout the year.

The areas for improvement, as noted in the documentation, are: teaching to the objective using approved district curriculum and strategies; teaching and disciplining without gender bias; and treating all students with dignity and respect, of which all core expectations for this district can be found in the handbook you received the first staff meeting of the year.

I will expect you and any representation you would like to attend with you, at a meeting in my office tomorrow at 4:00 p.m., December 21, XXXX. Any concerns about that meeting time should be made immediately to me so that an alternate time can be arranged. At that meeting I will verbally explain this letter and answer any questions you might have regarding Level B Intensive Assistance.

Ima Principal
Mrs. Ima Principal

Response Opportunity: I accept the guidance of the assistance team.

Mrs. Norapport

Mrs. Norapport came to the meeting with her union representative and after discussing questions relating to the appointment of the outside team, she decided to accept the assistance the team could provide.

Mrs. Principal contacted the Assistant Superintendent and told her that Mrs. Norapport had agreed to the assistance team. The Assistant Superintendent told Mrs. Principal to forward the signed copy of the recommendation and once it was officially received she would appoint a team who would then contact Mrs. Norapport.

After winter break, The team made an appointment with Mrs. Norapport and as assured, no reports were made back to the principal or assistant superintendent. During the time that the team was meeting with Mrs. Norapport there was no discernable difference in her behavior, complaints continued, and Mrs. Principal's observations continued finding no discernable improvement.

In was the end of March when Mrs. Principal decided to finalize this with a recommendation for non-renewal of Mrs. Norapport's teaching contract, effective at the end of the year. Great care needs to be taken in preparation for a notice of non-renewal. This letter needs to be a culmination of the documentation in a succinct form that could be used in a hearing, if needed. Mrs. Principal used the checklist that follows to help her organize her thoughts.

The following checklist might help when organizing personnel files used with marginal or incompetent staff. It can also be used as an administrator starts moving toward a more intense progressive discipline model.

Documentation Checklist

_____ Did you record the information promptly while the information was clear in your memory?

_____ Have you indicated the date, time, location, and witnesses to the incident?

_____ Did you clearly and factually record the behavior?

_____ Have you been totally objective?

_____ Have you cited specific rules or regulations that were violated?

_____ Did you indicate the specific impact on job performance and / or others?

_____ Did you record the consequences if the action or behavior is repeated?

_____ Did you list the prior intervention and response to previous inappropriate behaviors?

_____ Did you cite the employee's reaction to your or others' efforts to correct their behavior?

_____ Did you confer with your supervisor or the personnel office?

_____ Have you considered just cause and due process?

_____ Have you kept the personnel file organized for easy retrieval?

_____ Have you thought of each piece of documentation as a stand alone document that could hold up in a hearing? Is it clear, concise and yet complete?

The following is a letter that was drafted to share with the Assistant Superintendent prior to scheduling a meeting with Mrs. Norapport:

TO: Mrs. Norapport
FROM: Mrs. Ima Principal
            Anyschool USA
DATE: March 20, XXXX

Recommendation for Non-renewal

For the past year there have been continuous concerns that have been brought to your attention through discussion, memos, letters and observation reports, all of which are attached. Due to your unwillingness to change your teaching behavior I am recommending non-renewal of your contract.

The letter will go to the Superintendent this week, which will include the attached documentation. It will be his decision as to whether to continue this process by recommending non-renewal to the Board of Education. Any correspondence regarding that recommendation will come directly from the Superintendent's office.

If you would like to arrange a meeting with me regarding this letter, please make an appointment.

Mrs. Ima Principal
Mrs. Ima Principal

After the meeting with the Assistant Superintendent, who agreed that Mrs. Principal had the appropriate amount of documentation for this recommendation, the Assistant Superintendent met with the school district lawyer to review the final documentation and ask for any advice to make the preparation for non-renewal any stronger. He agreed that they were ready and suggested the letter be sent by registered mail to Mrs. Norapport.

The letter was also sent to the Superintendent who reviewed the documentation with the Assistant Superintendent and decided to proceed with the following:

Notice and Recommendation for Non-renewal of Contract

TO: Mrs. Gottsa Norapport
    1000 Anywhere Road
    Anytown, Anystate

FROM: Mr. Administrator, Superintendent
      Anytown School District
      Anytown, Anystate

DATE: March 28, XXXX

You are hereby notified that the Superintendent will recommend in writing to the Board of Directors of the Anytown School District at a regular board meeting that will be held on April 14, XXXX that your employment and teacher's continuing contract be non-renewed effective at the end of this current school year.

Following a decision of the Board of Education, the contract that will be non-renewed is between Mrs. Gottsa Norapport, a teacher, and the Board of Directors of the Anytown School District, located at Anytown, Anystate.

This notice is given pursuant to the provisions of Anystate Code section 279.15.

The recommendation to non-renew your contract is being made for the following reasons:

- Failure to teach to the objective using approved district curriculum and required district strategies.
- Failure to teach and discipline without gender bias.
- Failure to teach students with dignity and respect.

Copies of your evaluations and documents, which the Superintendent expects to present to the Board, are attached and represent documentation, which the Superintendent expects to present to the Board at a private hearing. The documents attached are incorporated with this letter to inform you at least five days before any private hearing, what information will be used. All documentation attached has been given to you in previous communications.

You have the right to a private hearing or to have the hearing open to the public. You must advise the Board, in writing, to the Secretary of the Board of Directors, if you choose to have an open hearing. This written notice must be received at least five days prior to the hearing or the hearing will be in private.

This Notice dated at 3:30 p.m., Anystate, this March 30, XXXX.

Anytown School District
Mr. Administrator, Superintendent

The process of working with marginal and incompetent staff is not easy to manage along with all the other concerns that daily represent responsibilities of an average educational leader, but they are very important to the well being and educational experience of the students.

Hopefully, this case study has helped the reader in gathering information on what an entire system of progressive discipline might look like in one scenario. If it is supportive, the goal for writing this book has been met.

ABOUT THE AUTHOR

Dr. Jo Campbell is presently the Assistant Superintendent for an urban school district in the Midwest. She has served in public education for nearly thirty years as a teacher, curriculum facilitator, principal, an assistant superintendent and national presenter.

She earned her Doctorate from Columbia University in New York City, her Masters of Science from Bank Street College and Parsons School of Design in New York City and her Bachelor's Degree from South Dakota State University in Brookings, S.D.

Printed in the United States
87361LV00002B/2/A